59

HAVE KIDS, WILL TRAVEL

THE COMPLETE HOLIDAY GUIDE FOR PARENTS

Photo: Dennis Friedman

SUSAN GROSSMAN is a single parent with an eight-year-old daughter. She has been a travel writer and photographer since her early twenties. Her first job in travel was writing and researching *Holiday Which?* reports for the Consumers' Association. She has been freelancing ever since, writing regular travel and consumer features for national newspapers and magazines, editing guidebooks, and broadcasting on travel for BBC Radio 4. Susan also writes video scripts and has presented TV programmes (BBC2's Food and Drink programme), as well as appearing as a travel expert on TV quiz shows, TVS Afternoon Club and BBC Breakfast Time. Other publications include *Self-Catering in Italy*.

HAVE KIDS, WILL TRAVEL

THE COMPLETE HOLIDAY GUIDE FOR PARENTS

Susan Grossman

CHRISTOPHER HELM
London

© 1987 Susan Grossman
Photographs © Susan Grossman
Line drawings by Mary Budd
Christopher Helm (Publishers) Ltd, Imperial House,
21–25 North Street, Bromley, Kent BR1 1SD

British Library Cataloguing in Publication Data

Grossman, Susan
   Have kids, <u>will</u> travel: the complete
   holiday guide for parents.
   1. Vacations—Handbooks, manuals, etc.
   2. Family recreation—Handbooks,
   manuals, etc.
   I. Title
   910.2'02   GV182.8

   ISBN   0-7470-1209-1

Typeset by Florencetype Ltd, Kewstoke, Avon

Printed and bound in Great Britain by
Billing and Sons Ltd, Worcester

CONTENTS

Acknowledgements

Part One: Pros and Cons of Travelling with Children

1. Introduction   3
2. How to Use this Book   6
3. Memories are Made of This: A child's eye
    view of holidays   8
    *Taking It In—Travelling Abroad—Opening
    Eyes—Sightseeing—Making It Last—Taking
    Pictures*
4. The Different Ages: What to do and when
    to do it   15
    *Babies—Toddlers—Three to Five's—Fives to
    Eleven's—Over Twelves and Teenagers*
5. Britain v. Abroad   29
    *Britain: The Seaside—Holidays in the
    Countryside
    Travelling Abroad: Food—Package Tours—
    Prices and Discounts—Free Holidays—Babies—
    Long Distances*
6. Where to Stay   36
    *Hotels UK—Hotels Abroad—B&B's,
    Guesthouses and Farms—Pubs—Self-catering*
7. Babysitting   40
8. Going It Alone   42
    *Single Parents—Children's Unaccompanied
    Holidays*

Part Two: Ideas for Holidays—Who Does What

9. Country by Country: Attractions for family
    holidays   49
    Britain—Europe and Further Afield

CONTENTS

10. Package Tours 69
Miniclubs—Tour Operators with Supervised Activities, Special Hotels or Facilities for Children

11. Beaches 72
Hazards—How to Find a Good Beach—Family Beaches Abroad

12. Winter Sun and Longhaul Destinations 76

13. Skiing 79

14. Cruises and Boats 81

15. Accommodation 83
UK—Abroad

16. Short Breaks 91
UK—Abroad

17. Self-catering 93
UK—Abroad—Before You Book—What to Take With You

18. Farmhouse Holidays 102
UK—Abroad

19. Camping and Caravanning Holidays 107
UK—Abroad

20. Holiday Camps, Holiday Clubs and Villages 112
UK—Abroad

21. Sports, Family Activity and Special Interest Holidays 119
UK—Abroad

22. Holidays for Unaccompanied Children: Sport and special interest 123
UK—Abroad

23. Working Holidays 129
UK—Abroad

24. Single Parent Holidays 132

25. Holidays for Handicapped Children 135
Guidebooks—Going Abroad—Organisations and Holiday Companies

Part Three: Travelling, Practical Advice and Information

26. Travelling 141
By Air—By Car—By Ship—By Train—During Pregnancy

CONTENTS

27. Holiday Health: Illness and accidents, treatment and prevention   159
Diarrhoea—Travel Sickness—Air Travel—Jetlag—Hot Climates—Sunburn and Heatstroke—Prickly Heat and Nappy Rash—Bites and Stings—Cuts and Grazes—Creeping Eruption—Immunisation —Falling Ill Abroad in Pregnancy

28. Holiday Headaches and Hazards   169

29. Holiday Books   171
Games—Languages and Foreign Places—Seaside and Countryside—Adventure and Sports—Maps and Things

30. Shopping Abroad   174
Shopping for Babies—Food Shopping—Medicines and Toiletries—Film

31. Packing   180
The Journey—Packing Bags Checklist—Medical and First Aid Kit

32. Passports and Holiday Insurance   184
Passports—Holiday Insurance—Medical Insurance

33. Reference Books   190

34. Booking Addresses and Tourist Offices   192
Holiday Contacts—Britain: Tourist Boards; Abroad: National Tourist Boards

Index   199

ACKNOWLEDGEMENTS

I would like to thank the following people and organisations for their help:

Professor Morley, Institute of Child Health and Dr Tony Waterson, Department of Child Health, Dundee; Thomas Cook Holidays, and all the Airlines, Tour Operators, Holiday Companies and Tourist Boards who have helped in providing information.

For Emily for travelling patiently

Part One

PROS & CONS OF TRAVELLING WITH CHILDREN

1

INTRODUCTION

'A sudden childish delight envelops me and the frontiers of myself disappear.' (Dame Freya Stark, *Alexander's Path*)

All of us at some moment in our lives have had that 'sudden childish delight' provoked by travel, whether it was from the thrill of touching down in a foreign place, seeing a beautiful sunset, distant snow-capped mountains or a vibrant foreign city.

What we often forget, when we are agonising over where to go, or how much it is going to cost, is that for children travelling is *always* exciting, however daunting the prospect for us.

But can a holiday *with* children be a holiday for parents too? A lot of parents think not, at least not as much of a holiday as it was before they had their children. It really depends on how you play it. If you carry on regardless and just let your children tag along to wherever you would have gone to without them, they might, or they might not, have a good time. One thing's guaranteed, if they don't, you won't—and it doesn't take much of a compromise to choose a holiday where all of you can enjoy yourselves. You just have to know where to find it.

You certainly don't have to spend all your valuable holiday time on your hands and knees making sandcastles, watching the baby have a siesta or keeping track of your teenagers. Most children (apart from little ones) will understand, if you tell them, that holidays are for everyone and that you need a break too. It may also surprise you to learn that children's best holidays are where they can see you're enjoying it too. So it's no use pretending you like trailing around a theme park if you don't. You can't fool kids.

Eating, drinking, sunbathing, shopping and sightseeing might rank high on your list of holiday pleasures, but for children, staying in a hotel, going abroad, swimming, having treats, stay-

3

ing up late and having you around all day long, usually means a lot more to them than what they get to eat or whether the sun happens to shine or not.

Travelling with babies and under fours *is* hard work although with young ones you do at least get a bit of time off when they sleep in the afternoons. You may panic at the thought of subjecting your toddler to mosquitoes and sunburn, and wonder if it's worth disrupting the baby's routine or spending money on someone who doesn't know the difference between Brighton and Bermuda. You may resent a lot of things until you suddenly realise what travel means to children and feel that 'sudden childish delight' as he sees the sea for the first time, feels the sand between his toes, leaves the ground on his first plane ride.

Children are, in fact, amazingly adaptable when it comes to travelling, they adjust more easily than we do to time changes, jetlag and hot climates. Babies and toddlers rarely object to disrupted routines, they just sleep when they're tired and demand feeding when they're hungry! To a baby the only important thing on holiday is you. It's us that do all the worrying. Not surprisingly, taking a child away from its familiar home environment is an enormous responsibility.

Disasters aren't the end of the world. To a child the best bits are often the things that go wrong: the delay at the airport when you all had to camp down in the departure lounge, the time the car broke down and you had to hitch a lift with a truck full of goats, the day the beachball floated out to sea and disappeared over the horizon, the afternoon when daddy almost fell off the back of a camel. Memories are made of this.

Travel itself is a stressful time for all of us, children included. For some the anticipation of getting there is sometimes more than they can bear. '*When are we going to get there*' is a record most parents have heard a million times over. Children have little appreciation of either time or distance. How they will behave on the journey depends on their boredom threshold, the supply of games and things to do, and how you tackle it. If you get agitated about delays, the chances are they will too.

Everyone knows that holidays don't always turn out to be as wonderful as you expect. For children the dream can be all too suddenly shattered. A nice sandy beach is no guarantee of happiness. Children can get just as bored on holiday as they do at home, and some take a while to adapt to new places. By the time the holiday is up most children are torn between not wanting to leave and looking forward to climbing into their own bed.

Taking children away is not cheap, especially the older they get, yet it needn't be prohibitively expensive. I've discovered a lot of holiday companies and hotels in this country and abroad keen to offer families good discounts and facilities.

This book is not a lecture on how to do it. It is a book based on my own experiences of travelling with my daughter, most of it in a professional capacity as a travel writer—much of it as a single parent on my own: in Europe, out of Europe and in Britain. I haven't trekked across India with her or hooked her to the boom of a yacht while I've sailed around the Med. but I have done most of the things that ordinary parents do with children and many of the things they don't. Along the way I've encountered a lot of helpful people keen to make travelling with a child as hazard free as possible.

It hasn't all been plain sailing. I've carted hundreds of disposable nappies to places where I could easily have bought them; taken Emily as a toddler on a disastrous motoring holiday around California; lost her on a beach in Cornwall; had to carry her around Paris because I forgot the buggy; and finally, at 8, had to worry as she packed her bags and went off on her own. Just as you begin to get the hang of it they don't need you any more!

I've worried about disrupted routines, unfamiliar food, having to carry luggage and a child (and I only had one!), missing planes, travelling at night, and falling ill in strange places. And I'm not alone. I've talked to perfectly intelligent, well-travelled parents who suddenly find themselves with a new baby and don't dare set foot out of the country. Yet I've talked to others who've never holidayed further afield than Margate and have then successfully taken three under 5's to India.

All I can tell you is that travelling with children is a bit like learning to swim or ride a bike. The whole thing is fraught with anxieties until you know how to do it. Once you've done it, that's it. Suddenly holidays with kids are at least as much fun as they ever were without them.

This book couldn't possibly have been written without Emily. For a child, travel is one of the most exciting things that can happen to them. I feel privileged to have been allowed to share in that experience.

2

HOW TO USE
THIS BOOK

I've called this book *Have Kids, Will Travel*, because a lot of parents have them and won't. Holidays with children can never be the same as holidays without them but there are ways of making travelling fun for all of you without compromising your budget or your behaviour.

This book is divided into three parts.

Part One is a general introduction to travelling with children, from babies to teenagers, with a look at the most suitable holidays for different ages and where to get the best discounts. But before you make any holiday decisions perhaps you should read the next chapter, on Memories Are Made of This, to find out just what travel really means to children, how much they take in and how much they gain from the whole experience. There's a chapter on the holiday possibilities for single parents, and the pitfalls for children who go off on their own. And there's a look at the most popular family holiday of all, the English seaside, and how it compares to taking the children abroad, on a package tour to Europe or to an exotic long distance destination. Where to stay is often a headache and an expensive one at that, but it needn't be: there are all sorts of possibilities in this country and abroad, from camping, or staying on a farm, to self-catering. Once you've sorted out what sort of holiday you want, Part Two will tell you how to go about arranging it.

Part Two deals with specific holiday ideas. You'll find holiday companies with big discounts, even for teenagers, hotel chains what will let your children share your room for nothing, hotels that welcome children rather than resent them, and tour operators with supervised miniclubs who offer everything from cots to cuddles! Whatever sort of holiday you choose, from caravanning to cruising, there are holiday companies that care about kids. The chapters on unaccompanied children's holidays and working holidays cover the questions you should ask before you send your child off on his own. As for holiday ideas, the Country by Country chapter includes all sorts of exciting things for children, in the UK and abroad, that you may not have known about, and ways and means of doing them. There are chapters on how to find a safe beach, ideas for activity holidays, where to find the best ski resorts, and suggestions for single parents and handicapped children. If you've had enough of hotels, and many families have, look up the chapters on self-catering holidays, farmhouse holidays, holiday camps, camping and cruises. And if you've had enough of going away to the same place at the same time as everyone else, there are ideas for winter sun and longhaul destinations, as well as short breaks for autumn, Christmas and half-terms.

Part Three is practical—general advice and information on travelling, packing, passports, insurance and holiday health. Getting to your holiday destination can be a major headache with a family in tow. This section deals with travel itself, the sort of help you can expect on planes, boats, trains and at airports. Should you travel when you're pregnant? What do airlines think of breastfeeding in public? Health on holiday is covered from common holiday illnesses like diarrhoea and travel sickness, to how children cope with hot climates and jetlag. In the Shopping chapter you can compare the costs of nappies abroad and find out which countries sell familiar brands of babyfood. There's a handy checklist for packing, and a chapter on travel books aimed at delaying the inevitable 'when are we going to get there?'. And, finally, there are names and addresses of travel companies who care enough about the needs of parents and children to make travelling *with* children—a holiday!

I've given names and addresses of companies, since the book wouldn't be much use to you if I hadn't. Hopefully, by the time you read this they will *all* still be in operation.

At the back of this book you will see forms for you to report on any holiday place you think is particularly suitable for families. Please say why and give full details and I will try and include it in future editions. I should also welcome comments on bad experiences, provided they relate to a specific product rather than a one-off experience that is unlikely to happen to anyone else. Comments from the children would be welcome too; please make sure they give their ages.

Apologies to all the people and places I've left out. Send me details if you think you warrant a place in the next edition or if any details of your organisation have changed.

3
MEMORIES ARE MADE OF THIS

'Travel, in the younger Sort, is a part of Education.' (Bacon)

Many of you may well wonder just what effect travelling has on children, and whether, when months later they seem to have forgotten all about the place itself, it was actually worth the money taking them abroad. Ask most children what they remember best about their holiday and they'll come up with an assortment of answers ranging from the day they spilt Coke on your camera to the doggy they fell in love with on the beach. But is that it? How much do they actually take in about different cultures, the countryside, people and lifestyles? Almost certainly a lot more than they let on about.

Most small children are aware of changes from their home environment whether you take them to the English seaside or to the Caribbean. What they do with that information is another matter. What is probably true is that the first impression is the most lasting one (which doesn't say much for foreign airports) and that things that happen towards the end of a day when they are tired are least likely to be remembered. Travel ranks well up in learning experiences. But a lot of what children take in is up to us. So what can we do to help?

Taking It In

Young children may remember incidents from holidays as early as 2 years old but most of their impressions will not do them much good in helping them pass their exams. Not until children are 9 or 10 are they able to think logically and observe accurately, yet at this age they are still young enough to retain that first

8

Memories are made of this?

sense of wonder that made Walt Disney remark that: 'Disney-land will never be completed as long as there's imagination left in the world.'

Most parents will know that you can't force a child to take in something that he doesn't want to. But learning is not just about collecting information and facts but the way we react to people and what's happening around us. On holiday the experience is shared with all the family. So a lot of what we remember is how we all got on together.

Barbara Roberts, a Yorkshire teacher, carried out a study of 300 children's long-term memories, a year after school visits to various museums and sites. Their ages ranged from 5 to 18, but regardless of how old they were she found that memories were triggered off by sensations, particularly taste and smell: 'a lot of the children's strongest memories were of what they had eaten for lunch.' She also found that the first events of a day were a lot more vivid, compared with later happenings—recall of 5–8 year olds of afternoon activities was pretty scant and the end of the day was a blur to most of the children. So, when planning excursions try and make them as early in the day as possible if you want the children to remember anything about them.

Another interesting factor was emotion; being away from home is often a tense and worrying time. But it seems when adrenalin is flowing, memories are strong. Lots of the children remembered outings where they were frightened (dinosaur museum), lost (however temporarily) or worried (losing something). They also remembered experiences that had been exciting, funny or incongruous.

'I remember when I was three daddy went down the water slide in France and got so wet he had to walk around without his shirt on for the afternoon.' (Stephanie, 7)

From her survey, Barbara Roberts believes that the more relaxed and comfortable a young child is, the less he is likely to remember. Which probably accounts for why minor disasters like the car breaking down, being delayed at airports and drop-ping your camera are some of the more memorable parts of the holiday for a lot of children.

Travelling Abroad—Observing

'The people were quite nice but we didn't understand them very much.' (Emma, 6)

What seems to be important is to help children observe and that's where you come in. Wherever you go the simplest way is to ask them questions and let them make the observations, rather than say 'look, they drive on the wrong side of the road here'. Try asking your children to tell you things that they notice are different from home. The chances are that if they observe whatever it is themselves it will sink in. It could take the form of a variation of 'I Spy'. As soon as you arrive ask them to point out things that are different, help them a bit by suggesting subjects like trees or buildings, smells and sounds. Observation does not come easily to most children as you have probably realised from the umpteen occasions when they lose something and you find it sitting at the foot of their bed.

For example, help them to notice that the roofs of the houses are made of thatch, that the policemen wear different uniforms, that cars drive on the opposite side of the road, and carts are drawn by mules—depending, of course, on where you are. And don't forget food. Children will soon realise when you stop for a snack that they can't necessarily get the same sort of ices, sweets or drinks as they insist on having at home. Trying out the local food on the one hand develops their palates but on the other quickly makes them realise that people the world over enjoy a lot of different tastes. They may well turn their noses up at tinned sardines at home, but fresh ones, that they've seen that morning, hauled in by the fishermen on the beach, may be quite another story.

'The first thing I noticed was that everyone was black.'
(Sarah, 6, St Lucia)

If things are very different, which they can be even on the Continent, don't assume they'll know why. Take Sarah's comment on her holiday to the Caribbean: 'the first thing I noticed was that everyone was black.' Why was it such a strong impression? Half her friends at school were black. Her mother had done a lot to try and forewarn her that the Caribbean was very different from home. They had gone to the library and taken out books on vegetation. She'd also told her how hot it was going to be and that they would have to be careful about the sun. What she hadn't realised was that Sarah thought everyone was black because they'd had too much of it! Once she'd expressed her thoughts it was easy to put her right.

Opening Eyes

'The houses are closer together to keep out the heat, and have shutters because it is cooler' (Jonathan, 11, Majorca)

Wherever you go on holiday you will probably want to take the children sightseeing to see something of local interest. However, before you go rushing off to see the nearest collection of antiquities, bear in mind that a museum could be the *last* place you should think of going to. Everything that's going on around you is of educational value and may be a lot more interesting!

Look around you. For the sake of argument, imagine you are

in a fairly typical holiday resort in, say, Italy. Here are a random selection of local images that your children could examine and use their imagination on, and possibly learn more about the foreign culture and day-to-day life of Italians than they would do visiting a museum. The scenarios in Italy might go something like this.

* Houses—spot the grannies in black, sitting out on chairs in front of the almost always open front doors, what are they doing? Do Italians not have washing machines, why are sheets always hanging off the balconies?
* Local children—they might see a school party in uniform, children playing outside and staying up late, older sisters looking after babies (without their mums); children abroad are often a lot more independent at a younger age.
* Vegetation—wherever you go you can try and identify what's growing in the fields and on the trees; very educational—even in Britain.
* Churchyards—some children have a morbid interest in death which could be turned to historical advantage. See if they can notice the difference between cemeteries here and at home (family graves in little houses, lamps and candles burning, photos); old cemeteries are particularly fascinating and the age at which the occupants died certainly highlight advances in medicine!
* Shops and markets—particularly food in windows. It won't take them long to work out that cake shops might account for the waistlines of Italian mamas and that little babies in Italy are very very important—just count how many shops there are with children's clothes in the window.
* Ads and roadsigns—tell you a lot about the people, language (easy words to learn) and possible hazards!
* People spotting is a good one, not just the local population and the way they might appear different to us, but other tourists! Recognising different nationalities if you are going abroad, or even trying to identify tourists if you are staying at home, cannot fail to increase your child's social awareness. Much fun can be had spotting different nationalities by the way they dress (hats and black socks on the beach for Eng- lishmen), three generations of a family (grannies live with their grandchildren) plus general hysteria and snazzy swim- suits for Italians, blonde, blue-eyed Germans, etc. etc.
* Occupation spotting is a good one. For example, you may be driving past a field and point out the farmer, the farmhouse and the children running around outside it. If you spend all your time in an office and that's the only work experience your child knows about, he may well be fascinated to catch a glimpse of the alternative lifestyle of a farmer.

Sightseeing

Children, contrary to most parents' beliefs, don't object to sightseeing on principle—as long as it is in small doses and they haven't already learned to hate it! Some may need a little persuading: with the promise of an ice-cream most youngsters will follow you anywhere. Explain what you are looking at (the more interesting and relevant to children you make it sound the better) and *why*, rather than just let them tag along behind you, and you may well have to drag them away! But there is a limit to how much you can expect a child to take in in a holiday atmosphere. Don't expect them to learn facts and dates out of guidebooks, as though they were in school. For years, educationalists have been thinking about how to interest children in museums. On the whole they believe that good displays and things children can participate in help—so long as they don't first have to read detailed instructions. There are numerous sights in Britain that try hard to help children enjoy them, from zoos that allow children to touch the animals to the production of simplified guides to draw their attention to the exhibits in a stately home (the National Trust are good at these). Worksheets aren't always considered to be a good idea; sometimes they take away from a child's natural interest and turn a visit into a competition.

Zoos are often particularly good with children. For example, at Drusillas Zoo near Littlehampton on the South Coast, there is an excellent exhibition for children on evolution, with simple knee high facts for them to read while touching and observing the animals in front of them. (Added to that there is one of the best adventure playgrounds I've seen anywhere with all sorts of inventive contraptions for them to test their bravery and skills.) Push buttons certainly appeal to most children (to start slides, models or engines) but the danger is that they may forget what they are supposed to be looking at and become obsessed with who gets to the button first! An educationalist once pointed out that, 'neither a tree nor a rabbit has push buttons, yet one can feel, hold and feed a rabbit, examine its colouring, observe its behaviour, and speculate on the structure and function of its anatomy'.

Observing things independently is often important to older children who often want the freedom to be allowed to stand and stare without being seen to be having a learning experience. Many of the older children, in Barbara Roberts' survey, remembered all too strongly that they weren't allowed to go off on their own to explore for themselves. There's nothing worse than taking in information if you're being watched!

Don't expect children of any age to enjoy being dragged around sights in the heat of the day when they are tired or when there's a better alternative. Try and make the whole outing fun even if it means allowing them a go in the playground outside or to spend their pocket money on rubbish from the souvenir shop before you leave. Whatever it's worth it will serve as a permanent reminder of the whole experience. Get them to keep guidebooks, postcards, even entry tickets. And don't start testing them in the car about what they've taken in—how would you like to have to describe the plot of a film to them every time you get home from the cinema!

Making It Last

Postcards and photos are obvious reminders of holidays, but so are other things. Children naturally pick up and collect things, from shells to beermats. Souvenirs, however inappropriate (and commercialised), probably help children remember things. It doesn't have to have anything at all to do with the place. If your child has chosen something to keep or has gone out and bought something with his own pocket money, the chances are he will be reminded of the holiday every time he catches sight of it. Don't force a child to keep a diary, it has been shown that putting pen to paper doesn't necessarily mean the experience has sunk in. On the other hand if your child is inspired to write something, even in the form of a letter to a grandparent, the chances are the experience has meant a lot to him.

Taking Pictures

Most children love the idea of taking pictures. Three isn't too young to start. If you can, get your child an instamatic camera of his own, buy a cheap film and let him get on with it. If he hasn't got a camera allow him a few shots with yours. Most children are pretty good photographers once you tell them what to do and they've seen a few rolls of film that they've ruined and been told why. Of course, you have to point out a few principles like it's not a good idea to face the sun, or take the photo with a tree growing out of grannie's head, and if they leave daddy's feet out of the viewfinder they won't appear in the picture. They've also got to be conscientious enough not to drop the camera in the sand or get it wet. Given the choice and no guidance, most children's holiday snaps would begin and end with the best friend they made on the beach or a stray cat poking at the dustbins outside your caravan. Never stop them from taking a picture they want to, but it won't do any harm to encourage them to take photos of their experiences: the place you stayed in, a place you visited, local friends, perhaps a few of those differences between home and away—with any luck their photos will provide them with tangible memories that in the future may trigger off others.

Travel for all of us is a learning experience. It is not something you can value in terms of the cost of a holiday. It might have cost you virtually nothing or the earth. To a child the experience is priceless.

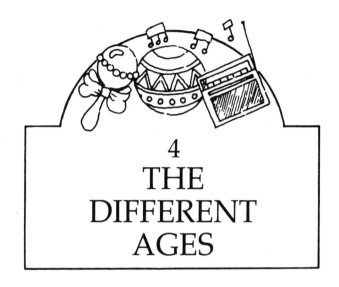

4
THE DIFFERENT AGES

Toddlers are horrendous to travel with, 5 year olds need occupying all the time, 9 year olds get bored, 13 year olds get off with the waiters. Babies are not as difficult as you might imagine —provided you're not planning to relax and enjoy yourself!

I am not pretending in this book that travelling with a child is easy, it isn't. It involves quite a lot of thought, not least of all about what sort of holiday is most suitable for your child, which depends to a great extent not only on his interests but also on how old he is.

Provided you want to do more than just let the kids tag along with whatever you are planning, the breakdown of different ages should give you a few ideas of the sorts of things that are suitable and where you can get the best deals.

If you've got a large family with children that fall into *all* the categories, don't give up. Lots of the ideas covered in the central section of this book are suitable for all of you.

Where I've suggested specific types of holiday or holiday companies, they will be covered in more detail in Part Two of this book.

Babies

'The baby was a bit of a pest on holiday he always likes to go to sleep halfway through the day so it stops us doing things, if you go in the car he climbs out of his car seat and if you go on a boat then he runs off.' (Claire, 8)

A lot of parents put off all sorts of holiday possibilities because

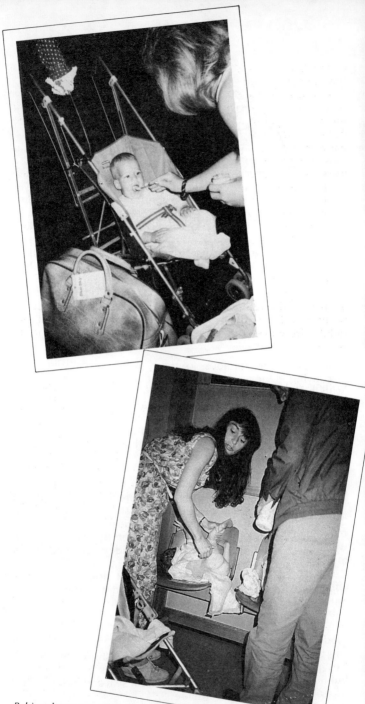

*Babies always seem to need
feeding and changing in inconvenient places.*

of the baby. Very young babies are the least demanding of travellers, and it's never too early to start!

So long as you're around most babies couldn't care less where they are. If you are planning a long journey or going abroad, infants are rocked to sleep by travel, don't usually suffer from car sickness, will normally sleep for a fair part of the journey and, while changing a baby in an aircraft loo is no mean feat, most airports, ferries, some cruise liners and Continental railways have good facilities for mothers and babies. If you are still breastfeeding, whatever you do, don't give up just before you go away. The baby will get your immunity to 'foreign' bodies, and having to take bottles and milk powder, teats and sterilisers as well as all the other paraphernalia is well worth avoiding if you possibly can. If you are bottle feeding, never fear, once you've survived the journey, many hotels and holiday companies in this country and abroad are only too willing to help!

On most holidays you don't have to pay for travel for infants. You can get skycots for long distance flights on scheduled airlines, and cots, and highchairs in hotels and self-catering properties all over the world. The only real drawback: you get a holiday from everything else except feeding and changing the baby!

Where to Go

Coping with a young baby on your own at home isn't easy, on holiday it can be worse. But if you have someone to share the feeding, changing and carrying around you'll be able to get a certain amount of enjoyment out of *wherever* you go. So choose a place you fancy. If you want cots, highchairs, early mealtimes, playgrounds, sandpits and shallow paddling pools you are best off with a conventional package holiday abroad or to go to an English seaside. If your baby is crawling it is best to go somewhere with fairly high standards of hygiene (not North Africa, for example), since your baby will inevitably be putting his hands in his mouth all the time. As for people to take the baby off your hands, you can even get holidays that come supplied with nannies and nurseries, both in the summer (see package tours, p. 69) and on skiing holidays in winter.

There are many intrepid parents who do not let parenthood affect their travelling at all! They happily take their babies hiking around Europe or sailing in a yacht. But for most of us, having a baby seems to curtail things or at least modify our holiday behaviour. Will the baby survive a hot climate? What about food? What about routines? Is it worth the money, especially if you're not going to get any free time to yourself? The answer is 'yes' it is worth the money. A baby may well alter your lifestyle but that doesn't mean you have to stop having holidays. There's a lot of fun to be had holidaying with a baby, certainly a lot more than staying at home because you think it won't be worth it!

Supplies and Equipment

There are, of course, certain bits of equipment you will need to take with you, wherever you are going, to make life easier (see packing, p. 180). Nappies are often a worry but babies all over the world wear them and you can buy disposables all over Europe and the States, although costs may be high (see shopping for nappies abroad, p. 174). Fortunately, in hot places, bare bottoms are acceptable and you'll need fewer disposables than you might have calculated for.

You can also get jars of babyfood abroad too, though brands may not be familiar ones. If your baby has a habit of spitting out things he doesn't know and like take your own packets with you.

As for equipment (see packing for full list), I always found the most important thing to take with me was a sling and/or a fold-up (preferably lie-back) buggy. If you're travelling by air, hang on to it right up to the steps of the plane, where the stewardess will then stow it away for you. There's nothing worse than a fractious baby trying to clamber all over the place while you're waiting for your luggage and Customs. With a buggy you can lead an almost normal life on holiday. The baby will usually sleep in it if tired enough (practise walking around the block at home first). I've parked a buggy in the poshest of places—once right under the table in a five star restaurant in Portugal, where my daughter snoozed through one of the best meals I've ever had. The buggy is also essential for evening shopping expeditions and parking in the shade on the beach—without it your time is limited.

It is also worth taking a baby sling, though again, your baby should be allowed to practise in it before you go away. You'll find it really useful if you are going to be walking about in crowded, cobbled, or uphill places where you can't push a buggy. Other essentials are a clip-on sun umbrella for hot places, a travel cot, and a net to keep off cats and insects. Mail order companies also sell all the holiday equipment you are likely to need including travel cots, clip-on highchairs, harnesses and travel bags (see packing).

Hotels and Package Tours

Mothercare have ventured into the package holiday market and have supplied hotels abroad that feature in the Lancaster Family First brochure with equipment from their stores, including cots, nappies, potties and creams (see p. 88). There are also nurseries on board Canberra Cruises on HCI holidays and at some Club Méditerranées.

Most hotels and tour operators that cater for families have cots (and highchairs) but abroad you should always check safety. Never leave a baby in a foreign cot without looking at the width of the gaps, both between the bars and between the mattress and where the bars start, and how sturdy it is. If necessary, use string, sheets or towels to fill in the holes. In an emergency it may be safer to let the baby sleep in a drawer! On package holidays you may have to pay for the cot at the hotel. Find out beforehand how much you are going to be charged: it should not be more than a few pounds per night.

Babysitting

Offers of babysitting aren't always totally satisfactory. In some package tour hotels they call it baby patrolling and all it involves is someone walking past or peeping into the room every half an hour or so. Baby listening in UK hotels isn't always so wonderful either—particularly if it involves a receptionist who isn't continuously at her desk! See chapters on package tours and accommodation.

The best advice I can give you if you are planning to travel with a new baby is not to worry about it. If you can, try and stick to regular feeding times, if you can't, let little ones sleep when they are tired and eat when they're hungry. The most important thing to a baby is you. The chances are if you're enjoying yourself, he will too.

Toddlers

Toddlers are wonderful people and terrible travellers. They are probably the most difficult age to travel with, although given that, there are still some parents who happily cart toddlers off trekking in the Himalayas. Personally I think you really do have to modify your holiday behaviour with toddlers because you have to watch them all the time.

If you want to get any sort of break yourself you will have to take someone with you who is willing to take over now and again—even a sensible older brother or sister is better than nothing. Or you could choose a holiday with a nursery attached. If you fancy doing something for yourself, perhaps a course during the summer, several universities have crèches where you can leave under 2's in capable hands while you get on with it.

For a conventional family holiday few parents would contemplate anything more arduous than a buckets and spades holiday at the seaside, British or otherwise; and how right they are. Choose a hotel with good facilities (see the ETB's *England's Seaside*) and a resort with good parks and playgrounds. Alternatively, try a farmhouse holiday.

You are asking for trouble if you try and embark on anything too ambitious. Stick a toddler in the back of the car for a motoring holiday and you will come back swearing never to do it again. Try taking a toddler to a tropical country where none of the food is familiar and the standards of hygiene leave a lot to be desired and you may well come back regretting every penny you spent. Take a toddler to a sandy beach in Devon or the Lido di Jesolo in Italy and you'll come back smiling. Toddlers like noth-

It gets easier the older they get.

20

ing better than to dig holes in the sand, fetch water with their buckets and stick ice-cream in their mouths. Very undemanding when you actually think about it!

Package Tours and Holidays Abroad

A few holiday companies have nurseries and baby clubs for toddlers at a number of hotels and resorts abroad where they can play and be looked after while you relax, Club Méditerranée and HCI among them. Lancaster Family First have special Mothers' Rooms (supplied with Mothercare equipment) in the hotels they use abroad. You can even take toddlers with you on a skiing trip, as resorts all over Europe have special kindergartens, staffed by trained English-speaking nurses and nannies, where they can sleep and be fed and changed, while you ski.

There are, of course, other possibilities. With a sturdy sling on your back you can take a toddler anywhere. If you want to hire a car abroad, several car hire companies will provide babyseats, and in countries like Norway, you can even get little seats on the backs of bikes. As for theme parks, I personally would wait a bit before taking a toddler to somewhere like Disneyland. I did it when Emily was 2. She loved it, but now can't remember a thing about it and keeps asking me when she can go again! On the whole, under 2's get cheap holidays, they can travel free on your lap on a plane (on charter flights) and often stay free too, although you may have to pay for the cot and any food.

Hazards

A toddler on the move is dangerous! There are hazards at almost every turn to a little person who has only just started to walk. It is very difficult finding a childproof holiday for a small person who is constantly on the go, scrabbling around after ants on the floor, popping out of the bedroom door for a quick explore of the fire escape. Toddlers need watching constantly, so a safe environment is essential.

Often it's the sort of things you couldn't have known about before you left home that prove to be the most hazardous. In Portugal once I discovered on arrival that the gaps in the bars on the balcony of our bedroom were wider than my daughter's head; in Sardinia the garden outside our villa was lovely but most of the plants were cacti; in Tunisia the sand got so hot during the day that the beach had to be out of bounds; in a holiday village in Spain our bungalow was about a mile from the main complex so we couldn't leave her to sleep, go and eat and keep an eye on her at the same time.

Always check the safety of cots abroad. Make sure there are no gaps for your child to stick his head through and that it is strong enough for a sturdy 2 year old. If you are travelling with Lancaster Family First they have Mothercare cots in a number of their hotels abroad and Wings-OSL's cots in their villas comply with British Safety Standards.

Equipment

Don't forget the buggy; it is the most important piece of equipment to take with you, unless you're happy to carry your child around with you. If you have a lie-back one, you may find your child can sleep in it so you can go out for dinner or for a walk in the evening without having to worry about babysitters. If you are going somewhere hot, take a clip-on sun umbrella. As for a potty, most mums who have just convinced a toddler to use it are pretty loathe to travel without it. The good news is that you can get an inflatable one! (see packing, p. 180). If your toddler is still in nappies you can get disposables virtually everywhere abroad (see shopping, p. 174) though you may be shocked by prices.

The toddling stage isn't a long one; while your child is in it take it easy on holiday, and save your money and energy for the next one!

Three to Five's

Three to 5 year olds aren't quite as bad as toddlers when it comes to travelling, but not a lot better. Most of them find it difficult to stay in one place for any length of time, except perhaps in a swimming pool. You should avoid any slow forms of transport unless you are prepared to stop often for loos, and snacks, and to let them run around.

The trouble with children of this age is that they need quite a bit of 'mum-made' entertainment. They may sit and listen for a while to songs or a story on a cassette if you are in the car but once you get there, their boredom threshold is quite low. So unless you are prepared to play games, or go off to theme parks, playgrounds and beaches continuously your luggage has to include bats and balls as well as books, toys, games and, of course, their favourite night-time companion.

Children of this age are less likely than older children to be impressed by their environment. Splendid sea views and exotic destinations will be wasted on most under 5's; most of them will get more excited by animals, beaches, theme parks, playgrounds and swimming pools.

Day Camps

If you want to get your under 5's off your hands for a bit during the school holidays, in Britain a number of holiday centres (like Dolphin) run *teenie* day camps for 3–5 year olds where children are well looked after and occupied on a daily basis. There may be one near your home. Activities tend to be fairly gentle; they may swim, go on walks, have competitions, do drama or paint. They are run like nursery schools and are a boon if you get desperate during the long school holidays. You can also usually get escorted coach travel from near your home. All you have to do at the end of the day is run a bath!

Teenie day camps for under 5's.

Holiday Camps and Theme Parks

Holiday camps and centres (like Butlin's and HCI) with their non-stop fairgrounds, playgrounds, and sophisticated swimming pools always go down well with small children. Some under 5's may be a bit daunted by the new wave machines and waterslides but most holiday centres also have separate paddling pools for less adventurous children. They also have entertainers and special menus in the restaurants. Four and five year olds will also appreciate theme parks. If you want to venture outside England try Legoland in Denmark or Disney World in the States.

Farms

Most small children, especially those that live in cities, appreciate a stay on a farm, so long as it has animals around. Many farms, both in this country and abroad are mechanised, so check first if you want more than a few cows in a distant field. Many farmhouse holidays also come with built-in babysitters, early suppers and sympathetic owners, so you can leave the kids sleeping while you go off to the pub in the evening.

Package Tours Abroad

If you are planning to go abroad as a family and want a straightforward beach holiday but also a bit of time to yourselves, many of the larger tour operators run supervised miniclubs for children at hotels abroad. Most offer a programme of fun and games, either in a special playroom or on the beach for children from 3 or 4 upwards. The number of hours of freedom you get varies; some operate for a couple of hours in the morning and the afternoon, others will take children off your hands all day. Playleaders are all English-speaking, though other children may be from other countries. As well as games, competitions, treasure hunts and bedtime stories they may also get sports tuition.

Prices

On the whole under 5's have no problem in getting discounts although some tour operators limit the number of holidays with high discounts, so you have to get in quickly when the brochures first come out. Often the best discounts only apply *outside* the school holidays so exclude a lot of families with older children.

Other Possibilities

You could take a cruise. Not such a mad idea. One cruise line offers substantial reductions for young children and has nurseries and playrooms plus a ship's nanny on board.

If you are planning to take your car abroad with you, children under 4 qualify for free travel with most of the ferry companies, so you could holiday cheaply staying in a *gîte* in France, or on a farm in Denmark. Camping is always exciting for this age-group, and there are sites all over Europe with pre-erected tents on them, plus on site couriers to take care of the children during the day. Several holiday operators will let you take children on camping holidays, free.

Or stick to the British seaside. Children aren't at the bucket and spades age for very long, you might as well take advantage of it while they are!

Fives to Eleven's

Children over 5 and under 11 are a lot of fun and appreciate where you're taking them. You can't fob them off with any old place, they want somewhere exciting and plenty of action!

While under 11's may be happy with ballgames on the beach or fishing about for tiddlers in a rockpool for a bit, you won't catch them doing any one thing for very long. The only fairly time-consuming activities for kids of this age are computer games and, if it's hot, the sea.

Activities—On Their Own

Children of this age are happiest with something to do on holiday. You can invent your own formula of entertainment or go somewhere where you know there's plenty of action. Or you can send them off on their own on a children's unaccompanied holiday. Camps up and down the country open their doors during the holidays and offer children a range of choices, from multi-activities to tuition in specialist subjects. They can choose to go on a daily basis or stay overnight. Either way *you* get a bit of a break.

Activities—As a Family

There are numerous holiday companies that run activity holidays for families, both in this country and abroad. You needn't all do the same thing: subjects cover a wide range of interests, sporting and otherwise. Or you could set off with your bikes or rucksacks on an organised itinerary.

Supervised Clubs—Package Tours and Holiday Centres

Abroad, tour operators run supervised clubs at hotels all over the Mediterranean. So while you are taking it easy the children have something to do. Pick carefully, a lot of 'miniclubs' may be too 'young' for your children. At this age they need specific activities, and may get bored if all that's on offer are fun and games. Choose a holiday company that either divides children into age-groups or offers a specific activity, like sports tuition or a Circus School (Club Méditerranée run them at several of their resorts abroad).

Other Possibilities

Camping holidays are also a good idea and you don't have to

At this age kids start going off on their own.

own as much as a tent peg to do it. Couriers on sites in Europe run special clubs with activities for children. You can also sometimes get sports coaching. Children travel and stay free whenever you want to go, even in the middle of the summer holidays.

This is the best age for theme parks, so if you can afford it head for Florida. If not, there are plenty of others in Britain and Europe. Look up the list (see p. 50) of the million pound developments that have taken place in Britain or try somewhere like Legoland in Denmark.

If you fancy renting your own apartment, bungalow, cottage or chalet, you might as well choose somewhere where there are things going on for the children. Holland's Center Parcs have excellent on site facilities with supervised activities, and holiday villages in Scandinavia also have a lot going on for children. If you opt for a holiday camp in Britain you're almost guaranteed not to see your children for hours on end. As well as a non-stop programme of activities most have sophisticated swimming pools with wave machines and waterslides.

Accommodation

For a conventional beach holiday abroad, Sol Hotels (a chain of Spanish hotels, see p. 89) feature in most of the package tour brochures. They have a lot going on for children at numerous hotels on the Costas and on the Balearic Islands. If you are booking a hotel independently, either in Britain or abroad, check on discounts. The larger hotel chains will often let children share your room for nothing.

Prices

If your child is nearing 12, this might be the last year for you to get a decent discount. There are tour operators who offer reductions for children over 12 but they are few and far between. The bulk of the discounts, especially if you are planning to travel on a scheduled flight, stop at 12. If you have a child with a summer birthday, and you're planning a trip abroad, make sure you travel before he lights his candles.

Over Twelves and Teenagers

By the time your children get to 12 you're in danger of their refusing to go away with you altogether. A prospect you might very well be looking forward to. On the other hand some teenagers keep on in there until 18 or so and expect you to pay for holidays year after year, even when they start work or want to go off without you on their own.

Taking older children away can get very expensive indeed. Most hotels, airlines and tour operators seem to think kids of 12 and upwards have some sort of private income, since over 12's get few concessions. With a large number of holiday companies, hotels and airlines, you pay the adult price or leave them at home.

Package Tours

There are, however, some tour operators who do extend their discounts to teenagers; the following are a selection of tour operators who do, with the upper age limits in brackets. Unfortunately, these age limits are not always applicable to *all* the holidays they offer, many only apply to certain hotels and destinations at specific times of year. Sometimes the reductions only apply to self-catering holidays. Check with the individual tour operator.

Blue Sky (14), Citalia (15), Cosmos (16), Enterprise (15), Global (17), Intasun (18), Jetsave (18), Lancaster Family First (16), Sovereign (19), Travel Club of Upminster (20). Also ferry companies (up to 16); and camping operators, Canvas, Eurocamp and Sunsites (up to 14 free); cruises Canberra (up to 20).

Doing Something

Older children are much more likely to be able to fit into your way of life on holiday. Several companies and hotel chains run specific family activities where they are unlikely to get bored and will also meet other children of the same age. The English Tourist Board's *Hobby and Activity Holidays* is the best source of ideas in England. Possibilities include: pony trekking in Wales, mountaineering in Scotland, barging through the canals of France, walking in the Spanish Pyrénées, painting in Provence or a visit to a working dude ranch in the States. At this age exploring cities becomes viable too, both to brush up their languages and for a bit of culture.

If they don't want to go away with you there are plenty of activity holiday centres in Britain (and special teenager weeks abroad) that run strenuous courses for teenagers keen to improve an existing skill or to learn a new one. Subjects range from every conceivable sport to learning a language or more about computers. There are music, dance and drama workshops, sailing and survival courses. Some involve roughing it a bit, perhaps living in tents or on board a boat, others are based in schools or universities. If they go on their own they are guaranteed to make friends.

Working Holidays

Once children reach 16 or so, they can volunteer to help out on conservation projects in Britain or go on various working holidays abroad, anything from being an au pair in Norway to helping handicapped children have a holiday at the English seaside.

Accommodation

Don't pay full price in a hotel until you've checked that there isn't one nearby where teenagers can share your room for nothing. A lot of the hotel chains in this country and abroad (including the States) will accommodate 16 or 18 year olds free. Bear in mind though, that big kids may well not want to share with you; not only will they almost certainly cramp your room, but you'll almost definitely cramp their style!

5
BRITAIN V. ABROAD

Britain

The Seaside

Going on holiday to the seaside is the most popular choice in Britain for family holidays. But don't assume that your children are automatically going to have a wonderful time, especially if they've never been to the sea before. For little ones, the sea can be quite frightening as the waves lurch over their feet and quite cold too! Children of 5 and upwards usually know what to expect and love the seaside, although they too can shiver in the wind, get too hot in the sun and get jolly irritable if they get too much sand in their pants or between their toes. Most children need to be kept occupied and can run out of things to do on beaches and get bored just as quickly as anywhere else.

You and I probably spent most of our holidays at the English seaside—and although we couldn't always have enjoyed it, if you think back you can probably only remember the good times. We didn't care about the weather (can you remember being cold?). Our mums and dads may have been huddled up in coats behind the windbreaks but we were running naked to the sea—heading for that spray of salt as the waves hit the beach. Our holiday memories are made of miles and miles of bumpy sand at low tide, donkey rides and competitions on the beach, skidding on seaweed and fishing for tiddlers in rock pools, bike rides along the cliffs and brass bands on the prom. We didn't get mosquito bites, sunburn or diarrhoea from foreign food. We sent rude postcards of busty ladies to our grannies, spent our pocket money on bumper cars, toffee apples and rock and captured it all on our Brownie 127s.

These days the essential ingredients are still the same, but what has changed is that there's a lot more besides. Resorts have moved with the times and now provide a huge number of things to do, regardless of the weather. Vast sums of money have been poured into seaside resorts: £15 million was spent on Blackpool's Sandcastle, which opened in June 1986—Europe's first indoor resort with pools, waterslides, entertainment day and night, children's play areas and garden terraces; £650,000 was spent on Scarborough's Kinderland, one of the most sophisticated children's adventure playgounds in England. Even Bournemouth has tried to change its retirement image and attract families by spending £18 million on new facilities including an indoor leisure pool with a wave making machine (certainly not designed for the grannies in the deckchairs on the prom.).

The beauty of the English seasides is that they are all different: big and brassy if you want them that way, stretches of unspoilt coastline where you can't buy so much as an ice-cream if you don't. And there's plenty more to a seaside holiday than just buckets and spades. Within easy access of any of them are river estuaries teeming with wildlife, country parks and farm trails, zoos and bird sanctuaries, monuments and earthworks. You'll find ships to explore that tell tales of battles at sea, castles on clifftops, smuggling museums, collections of steam trains, toys, clocks, armour and costumes, stately homes to explore and a whole list of special events, fairs and attractions going on throughout the summer all over Britain.

If you haven't fixed your seaside holiday in England, the English Tourist Board publish *England's Seaside*—a guide to 100s of seaside hotels and guesthouses.

Holidays in the Countryside

Of course you don't have to go to the seaside, there are plenty of other holiday possibilities in Britain, from pony trekking through a National Park to taking a boat through the inland waterways. There are activity holidays based at public schools and universities, family holiday courses to follow, farms to stay on, holiday centres with non-stop activities and cottages to rent deep in the heart of the countryside.

Once you've decided where you're going it is well worth finding out what is going to be happening in the surrounding area (including things like the nearest livestock market, special events, shows, etc.). There's nothing worse than finding out, after the event, what you've missed. Contact the relevant regional tourist office (see pp. 196–7) or Tourist Information Centre. They will send you detailed information of places of interest, a calendar of events, maps, and information about everything in their area. Most of it will be free. Or call in as soon as you arrive.

There are numerous guidebooks and brochures produced by

the Wales, Scottish and English Tourist Boards packed full of holiday ideas and how to go about booking them (see pp. 190−1). For starters, get hold of a copy of the free brochure, *England Holidays*, produced by the English Tourist Board. Most major travel agents and Tourist Information Centres will have it. Do the same for Scotland and Wales. Then contact the regional or local tourist board of the area you are interested in going to for more detailed information.

As far as children are concerned Britain can be just as exciting a holiday destination as anywhere else in the world.

Travelling Abroad

'Everybody, if they know you or not, smiles and says hello' (Lucy, 5, Spain)

Travelling to a foreign country may not make much of an impression on a young baby or toddler, but as soon as a child begins to notice things, he will be well aware that you are somewhere different. England probably has the least sympathetic attitude to families travelling with children than any other country in the world! And, as Lucy so rightly noticed when she went to Spain, as soon as you get out of England even strangers talk to you—provided, of course, you've got kids!

A couple of years ago Thomas Cook carried out a survey of over 500 children aged 8−12: 92 per cent of them said that they would prefer a holiday abroad to a holiday in this country. Most said they would rather go somewhere 'different' next year and had very firm views as to where it should be. One in four specifically mentioned Disneyland. Needless to say only 16 per cent felt they had any say in the matter. What they liked doing best was 'staying up late' and 'swimming in a pool'. What they found most boring were 'shopping and sunbathing'. Not a lot of people know that!

Holidays abroad are generally more expensive than holidays at home but apart from the cost there's no reason why you shouldn't go abroad with children, whether you have a newborn baby (you can get nappies and babyfood everywhere) or a teenager of 18. Travelling to countries outside Europe needs a bit more thought, but is perfectly feasible.

Food

'The only thing that's English about Italian food is spaghetti Bolognese.' (James, 5)

Food abroad *is* different. And a jolly good thing too. There's nothing more likely to put a spanner in the works of a fussy eater than to be faced with a plateful of food he doesn't even recognise! Sixty-four per cent of the children in Thomas Cook's survey said they liked trying different foods while on holiday, although quite a few of them had clear preconceptions about what they might get to eat. Over a third of them thought spaghetti Bolognese and lasagne were 'horrid', but most horrid by far were octopus (85 per cent), frogs' legs (87 per cent) and snails (89 per cent).

However ardent you are at home about brown bread and raw carrots, nutritional diets on holidays often have to go by the board. Most children look forward to pizzas, hamburgers, fish fingers, chips, ice-cream and endless Cokes when they go on holiday—and get them! If you find a children's menu in a hotel abroad, even if the local dishes are totally unfamiliar your children will be offered hamburgers, chips and ketchup, from the Caribbean to Denmark. The States have the most spectacular empty calories on menus: enormous piles of pancakes with maple syrup (for breakfast), mountainous ices covered in nuts and chocolate, free lollipops to take away with you.

Try and encourage the children to experiment with new food. You could begin by pointing out to them that although it is unfamiliar it is what the local children eat. Trying new foods might not go down too well at home, but on holiday children are much more likely to be adventurous. By doing so mealtimes may turn out to be a lot easier once you get back home.

In France, Italy, Spain and Portugal, restaurants are usually quite happy to bring small portions of whatever you're eating for the children to try, and charge half price (sometimes nothing) for them. Often children are whisked away into the kitchen and come back with their faces covered in ice-cream, such is the delight of waiters at meeting foreign children.

Eating out abroad can be expensive. Thomas Cook did a survey of restaurant prices in a number of their holiday destinations (summer 1986) and found that: Crete was the cheapest place to eat out followed by Corfu, Majorca, Minorca, the Costa del Sol, and Gran Canaria where the cost for a meal for two was much the same as it is here. More expensive than here was Lanzarote, then: Portugal, Cyprus and Madeira. Ibiza and Tenerife were the most expensive countries to eat out in.

If you know your children will only nibble at the food put in front of them abroad do not buy a holiday package with food included that offers them little reduction.

Package Tours

A package holiday is the easiest way to do it. All the arrangements are made for you and if you pick carefully you can find yourself a holiday that provides everything you need for the children: cots, highchairs, babysitters, shallow paddling pools, swings, playrooms and other children for them to play with. Most of the larger tour operators run miniclubs and activities for children of all ages at certain hotels where they can be supervised for hours at a time, so you can get some free time to yourselves.

You aren't restricted to a conventional hotel on a Costa either, the choice is enormous. You could: self-cater on a farm in Denmark; take a horse-drawn caravan through Ireland; stay in a holiday village in Italy; go skiing in Austria; rent a chalet in Switzerland; stay on a kibbutz in Israel; or potter along a canal in France.

You may be surprised at just how many different possibilities there are on the pages of holiday brochures and most of them perfectly suitable for families.

Once you have found a resort you are interested in, and a specific hotel, compare brochures. Often more than one tour operator will go there. Ask a good travel agent to tell you the names of all the operators and then compare not only price, but the times of flights, whether your room has a seaview or balcony and how generous their discounts are for the children (see below). If the travel agent says he doesn't know which other tour operators go there, ask him to look it up in his holiday guides (like those published by St James Press) which he will have under the counter.

It is quite common to find different prices from different operators for what looks like the same holiday, to the same hotel, in the same week.

If you don't fancy a package you might want just to get in the car and drive or get on a plane and then hire a car in a foreign country. Hardly surprisingly, there will be attractions for children wherever you decide to go (plus a carseat for the baby in your hire car and hotels that will let children share your room for nothing). Hopefully the chapter Country by Country will suggest places for you to go to and things to do you might not have known about.

Prices and Discounts

Package tours are undoubtedly the cheapest way of taking your family on holiday. If you shop around you can find tour operators that will take your children away for nothing. Some give excellent reductions to one child but very little for a second one, some extend their offers to larger families, while others restrict discounts to certain times of year or to specific hotels or resorts. You have to read the brochures carefully. To qualify for reduced prices at any time of year, children almost always have to share your room.

Sharing your room with your children on holiday may not sound like such a dreadful thing, if you're used to it and the room is big enough. But if you are not used to it and the room isn't, there's nothing guaranteed more to make you all hate each other by the time you get home. If it is very hot, hotel rooms abroad can get unbearable and while most hoteliers are perfectly happy to squash yet another 'z' bed into a corner, you may not be so happy leapfrogging down to breakfast. Before you accept that wonderful price reduction, bear in mind what you'll have to put up with. Some tour operators will give children a small discount (Thomson) if they want their own room.

Price reductions are usually based on one or more children travelling with two full fare paying adults. Sometimes they are based on one adult (important for single parents, see p. 132). Usually the biggest reductions are early and late in the season with smaller discounts during July and August. But there are exceptions.

Since children's reductions are such a strong selling point, tour operators change their policies not only every year but almost every season too. In general, children under 2 travel free and children from 2 to about 11 qualify for the best reductions, so it's financially worth planning holidays *before* a twelfth birthday if there is one looming. But discounts do exist for older children, with some companies right up until they are 16, 18 and even 20. If you are planning to self-cater rather than stay in a hotel, most tour operators extend their reductions to teenagers.

Free Holidays

Some package holiday tour operators use free offers for children to lure customers. Do not get excited. Most of these offers only apply if you are prepared to take the children away during term time and there are usually only a limited number of holidays to a limited number of destinations available. Unless you get the brochure as soon as it is published (for summer holidays, in the autumn of the year before) you will have missed out. There are also free holidays offered during the winter.

Babies

Although babies and under 2's can get free air travel (they have to sit on your lap on the plane) most tour operators state in their brochure that you will be charged a small amount for a cot and any food they consume at the hotel. Check in advance how much this small amount is likely to be. Around £2 a day is about as much as you should reasonably expect to pay. Some tour operators also charge infants a small amount to cover security and airport tax.

Long Distances

Children adapt better than we do to long distances. They recover from jetlag quicker and adjust to changes in climate in less time than we do. They also have bags more energy, so when you are flagging they are carrying on regardless. I took Emily to Los Angeles on a night flight when she was 1, petrified that she'd want feeding just as the luggage was coming off the conveyor belt, and certain that she'd want to go to sleep when I was trying to mobilise her and the suitcases, and then wake up and start toddling when I was dropping with exhaustion. I needn't have worried. On the day we travelled she decided to do without sleep altogether. When we finally arrived we passed out together, woke at the same time and after about 24 hours had adjusted to the LA clock. You can't stop children sleeping when they're tired, but you can wake them up after a bit and try and get them into the new time gradually.

Since then she's trailed around after me in the Caribbean, in the Sinai Desert and in Africa. Fortunately, the only ill-effects have been a nasty mosquito bite on her eyelid—and that could have happened anywhere. What you do have to bear in mind if you are travelling longer distances is health precautions. Never drink tap water and watch what you eat. For many countries outside Europe it is advisable to have vaccinations against local diseases. Children routinely will have been inoculated against many of them already.

There are possibly a few places I personally wouldn't venture to with a young child (but plenty of parents would). I wouldn't go to Kenya on a game drive with an under 7 year old; I wouldn't attempt long walks in the bush or jungle with under 10's; nor would I take children or a baby to places where it is very, very hot or very dirty. You can't stop a baby putting its hands in its mouth (say in North Africa, for example).

If long distances to you mean good quality hotels which you don't plan to leave for very long, I can't think of anything anywhere, apart from the cost, that would put me off. There's absolutely no reason why you shouldn't take children to the Caribbean, for example.

Whether you decide to stay in Britain or go abroad, from the Thomas Cook survey it emerged that one of the most important things for children on holiday was to have their parents around all day long, and that they really appreciated their joining in games and activities. They were also grateful for all the extra treats and pocket money. Most important of all to a lot of them was whether or not their parents were enjoying it too!

'My mum's different on holidays, she's nicer, she's more cheerful, she's got more money and she even goes in the water!' (Sally, 12)

Don't forget your costume!

6
WHERE TO STAY

The choice of accommodation on holiday if you are taking the children with you is probably as important as where to go, and how to get there. And the choice is large: hotel, guesthouse, pub, farm, cottage, log cabin, villa, tent, caravan, aparthotel, among them.

Hotels—UK

In Britain, a large number of hotels actually refuse to accommodate young children, something that is unheard of on the Continent. Even hotels that accept children can make families feel distinctly uncomfortable, particularly if their offspring shatter the great British silence at breakfast, or thunder down the corridor to your bedroom. Most parents will have experienced having to keep their children firmly under control in hotels at some time or other; will have been embarrassed at having to stop them from talking too loudly, screaming with excitement, sliding down the banisters, and generally enjoying themselves. Fortunately, and because the situation has become so bad in recent years, a number of guidebooks have now been produced that list hotels that actually welcome children. This means that you shouldn't have to set foot inside a hotel that doesn't provide everything you and your family could need, from cots and highchairs to early suppers and babysitting. It is also a relief to discover that a number of the larger hotel chains in Britain, also encourage families—and price their room rates accordingly. It is easy to spot a hotel that doesn't much like children, they won't give any reductions, don't have a tin of beans in the kitchen and haven't the faintest idea of how to warm a baby's bottle.

Hotels—Abroad

Continentals love children, especially other people's. Italians are perhaps the most demonstrative about it, there's almost nothing they won't do to make your child happy. Even to the extent of removing it from your presence for long periods of time. A hotel holiday based abroad will generally not leave you feeling embarrassed or uncomfortable. What you may have to contend with if the hotel has few facilities, is bad behaviour and boredom. Children do not like being restricted to specific meal-times, and unfamiliar foreign food. They like to be able to run around, eat when they are hungry and have somewhere to play.

If you want to go on a package tour, many tour operators have a large number of hotels that are suitable for families. Thomson, for example, highlight in their brochure hotels that are specific-ally good for children (early mealtimes, cots, highchairs, play areas and paddling pools). Lancaster Family First, in conjunction with Mothercare, have supplied the hotels they use abroad with special mother and baby units. Sol Hotels in Spain are excellent for families and most of the bigger tour operators use them. They have specific floors of hotels entirely devoted to children's needs. If you want to find out more about a hotel in a tour operator's brochure, either ring the tour operator direct or ask your travel agent to look it up in the *Agent's Hotel Gazetteer*, which he should have under his desk.

If you want to holiday independently and book your own hotel it is not so easy to find one that is suitable for children. In Part Two of this book under accommodation you'll find: a list of hotel chains where you'll be welcomed as a family, the guide-books that include hotels with good facilities for children, and advice on how to find a good and cheap hotel abroad. You can also get information from the National Tourist Board of the country concerned. In America almost all hotels and motels fix their prices on the room, not the number of people in it. And since it is quite common for hotel bedrooms to have two king size double beds in them, travelling with a family can be quite economical!

B&B's, Guesthouses and Farms

One of the alternatives to staying in a hotel is to opt for a small guesthouse or private bed and breakfast accommodation. This is obviously cheaper than a hotel but it has disadvantages. In Britain, most landladies are terrifically friendly at breakfast but many don't much like the kids running around the house during the day. On the other hand there's usually no problem about getting early suppers, since everyone automatically eats at around six or seven. Farms are a better idea with a young family as you are more likely to be able to hang around during the day, especially if there is a farmyard full of animals. Farmers' wives are pretty good about coping with foodfads and fussy eaters too, even children who hate eggs have been known to change their minds if they've been able to help themselves to them straight from the hen! Watch out though if your children are semi-vegetarians, they may refuse to eat meat altogether, having seen baby lambs, chickens and piglets frolicking around the place. Trying to explain to young children why we eat meat at all can be a tricky one! Farmhouse holidays are not just restricted to England, you can stay on farms all over Europe (see p. 102).

Pubs

Although there are some pubs that make an effort to encourage families and have family rooms and swings on the back lawn, on the whole staying in a pub is not a brilliant idea for a family, particularly as there are other, just as cheap, alternatives.

Self-catering

Millions of families opt for self-catering year after year. Not only is it a sensible choice if you are taking children away but a cheap one too. What self-catering does is to give you freedom. Freedom to do what you like, when you like for the duration of the holiday.

Most people who self-cater don't spend their holiday slaving over a hot stove. They simply use the kitchen for the odd meal, probably breakfast, and for preparing easy meals for the children. You can heat up milk for the baby when you like, make high tea for toddlers in the middle of the afternoon and generally cope much more easily with fussy eaters. Every parent knows how much money they've wasted by feeding their children in restaurants with food they've just picked at and left. On the whole a self-catering holiday is cheap and a lot more relaxing than staying in a hotel.

You have a very wide choice, both in this country and abroad: you can self-cater in a flat, in a castle, in a tent, caravan, villa, flat, log cabin, bungalow or boat. You have the choice between a property that's fairly private, perhaps in a village or small seaside resort, or you can opt for a large village complex where there may be hundreds (thousands in the case of some complexes in Spain) of properties, all identical.

If you decide to go for a property that's all on its own there are disadvantages in that you may be some way from the nearest facilities (pub, restaurant, beach, shops). With this sort of property you almost always need a car. If you choose one of the bigger complexes (could be anything from a caravan park to a cluster of up market villas) there will almost certainly be other kids of the same age for yours to play with. For parents who value a bit of time on their own this can be important enough to put up with other people being around! Added to that, most big complexes have a wide range of organised activities going on, although you don't have to join in. You might get: sophisticated swimming pools, tennis courts, bikes to ride, a disco, restaurants, supervised playrooms and playgrounds, watersports, shops, a launderette and evening entertainment. In fact everything and more that you might expect from a hotel, only if you are self-catering you stick to your own timetable.

I've picked out some of the better deals and the more interesting holiday companies in the chapter on self-catering (see p. 93), divided into UK and abroad. If you plan to do it abroad you can often take the children for nothing, even during the summer holidays and particularly if you are taking your own car. While reductions on hotel-based package tours are often only for children under 11, and only apply to the first child, on self-catering holidays reductions are usually extended to older children and may apply to your whole family.

Provided you don't spend your whole time cooking or clearing up, self-catering is about the cheapest and most practical sort of holiday with children in tow!

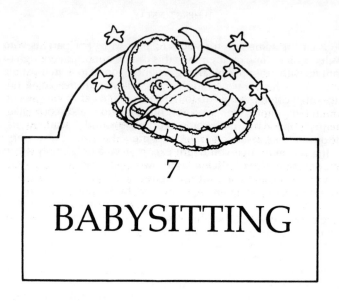

7

BABYSITTING

Babysitting is something I personally think rarely works out satisfactorily on holiday. First of all, most young children are pretty loathe to be left alone in a hotel room and many will not let you leave the room until they are well and truly asleep (it's no use creeping out they always hear you). On the Continent, of course, families keep their children up with them during the evening and everybody has a 'siesta' after lunch. Fine in principle, except that some children will not sleep after lunch however hot it is, and although some parents don't mind their children being up with them in the evening, others prefer a bit of time to themselves once the kids have gone to bed.

It may be necessary at some point in your holiday to enlist the help of a babysitter. Most larger package tour companies can arrange one-to-one babysitting for you, but on the whole only offer a 'baby or kiddie patrolling service'. This is not babysitting. What it entails is a young girl (often a rep.) wandering past your hotel room every half hour or so to listen outside the door to establish if your baby or child is crying. Sometimes they will go into the room, if you give them a key and tell them in advance where you will be. If the child is crying, she will appear at the door of the dining room, hold the child in the air to be identified and hand him over! The chances that your child will wake up and cry for a full twenty minutes before being 'patrolled' may not leave you relaxed enough to enjoy your evening, especially if you are out on an excursion. Some operators limit this facility to a certain age-group, often 2 to 12 and only until midnight, after which they make a small charge. It is often better to arrange for a proper 'full-time' babysitter. Your tour operator's representative may do this for you or you can ask a chamber maid, a friendly waitress or the hotel reception will find some-one for you. In some places it is quite difficult to find a young local girl who speaks English, and she may not be able to reassure your child if you have disappeared from the premises. The other factor is that your room may be tiny, and your child may not be too happy with a babysitter sitting, with the light on, next to its bed. Rooms with balconies are the best.

The most successful 'evenings off' I've had abroad are when my daughter has befriended another child. This is really only possible from about 4 upwards. We have let them share a room to go to sleep and taken it in turns to 'listen' at the door. If there are two or more of them in the same room together a) they'll giggle themselves into slumber and b) can give each other moral support in coming out and finding you.

8
GOING IT ALONE

Single Parents

'If you're the only single parent amongst 50 or 60 married couples, you're going to have a lousy, awful, rotten, lonely, holiday.' (Single mother of 3)

One in eight families in Britain are headed by one parent, 85 per cent of them women. A total of one and a half million children. For more than half of them holidays are out of the question. But even when a one parent family can afford a holiday there are other problems.

Travelling alone with a child in our couple-geared society can be a pretty daunting experience. The statistics might say that one in three marriages end in divorce, but all single parents know that on holiday they always seem to be in a minority of one. Problems seem to get magnified when you have to take sole responsibility for getting yourself and a child to a place. Once you're there you face another set, not least of all loneliness. There's absolutely nothing worse when you're holidaying alone with a child than to land smack in the middle of happy family land!

Since finance is often very important, how much the holiday is going to cost becomes the first problem to sort out. You probably feel just as entitled to a discount for your children as any parent. But you don't always get one. When it comes to prices, most hotels and tour operators usually only give reductions to children if they share a room with *two* full fare paying adults. Not much help to an adult travelling alone.

There are, however, some who appreciate the needs of single parents and are prepared to give reductions for one adult travelling with one or more children, only there is often another drawback; the reductions often only apply *outside* school holidays, which means that unless you have under 5's you have to take them out of school in order to get your discount.

You may not be bothered about whether you meet other people on holiday, but it is usually important for your children to, especially if you want some sort of break yourself. The best holidays are where there are other children of the same age as yours around, although some children can suffer pangs of guilt at abandoning a parent: 'I don't like to leave mum on her own. If I meet other people I always feel bad about going off with them if she hasn't got anyone to talk to.'

Dads who take their children away generally don't mind very much who they are surrounded by during the holiday—or whether or not anyone other than a waiter talks to them. For dads who seldom see their children the most important thing is to spend as much time with them as possible. Most single fathers I've spoken to don't seem to care if there's decent company for themselves. Even if there was they say, there wouldn't be any time to do anything about it. Time with the children is all too short.

Finding someone to talk 'innocently' to on holiday isn't that easy either. If you talk to couples, sooner or later they get it into their heads that you must be after one of them; if you talk to singles you stand the chance of having to wriggle out of a difficult situation because they think you're interested. Many single parents wouldn't dream of encouraging a holiday romance with the children around. If it happens, that's another matter. Sitting at a bar on your own after the children have gone to bed isn't much fun either. Most parents holidaying alone with their children tend to go to bed with them, whether it's at two in the afternoon for a siesta, at six with an exhausted toddler or at ten with a teenager.

So what holiday choices do you get as a single parent? You can book yourself an ordinary holiday where you may or may not meet other parents on their own (and run the risk of finding that 'all the world's a couple'). You can choose a holiday specifically for single parents (good for the children in that they'll find lots of others in the same boat, but possibly not so good for you if you don't happen to like them). You can opt for an 'activity' or 'special interest' holiday and get on with doing things (so you don't sit around feeling left out and lonely). Or, and I personally, think this is the best bet, you can go on a holiday, in this country or abroad, that has supervised activities for children (perhaps a holiday camp, somewhere like Club Méditerranée or a conventional package that has a miniclub at the hotel). That way you and the children get a break from each other and the chance to enjoy yourselves.

Holidays on your own with children aren't easy. The chapter in Part Two should direct you to sympathetic hoteliers and tour operators and give you some ideas you may not have thought of.

Children's Unaccompanied Holidays

'I kept getting thrown in the swimming pool with my clothes on, it was wonderful.' (Mandy, 8)

How would you feel if your 8 year old came home from school one day and announced that she was going off on holiday on her own to paddle a canoe, jump off a clifftop backwards, shoot the odd rifle and learn to ride a motorbike? Justifiably petrified I'd imagine, like I was. But my daughter's done it several times now and loved it. Thousands of children from 3 upwards take off to children's holiday centres all over Britain every year, either on a daily basis or as residents for a week or longer at a time.

The number of companies offering this sort of holiday is growing all the time, although a relatively small proportion of British children go off on holiday on their own, compared to about three-quarters of all European children and some eight million Americans.

So how do you make sure your children will be in safe hands? Unfortunately there are no laws governing this sort of holiday and anyone can open a centre. All you can do is to select a company that has been around for a bit, check with other parents on its reputation, and satisfy yourself that the staff are qualified to teach the activities they have on offer.

Fortunately a large number of companies have proved that children have a wonderful and safe experience—even if they do come home grubby and exhausted.

Day Camps

'I might cry when I get on the bus, but I'll only be pretending.' (Christian, 3, day camp)

There is a way of trying an unaccompanied children's holiday out, before packing your child's bags and sending him off to live-in for a week. A number of the larger companies have introduced day camps. These are held in schools and holiday centres up and down the country, and there may well be one near your home. Obviously if you live in a remote part of the country this won't be a possible option for you, but large areas of Britain are covered and it is certainly one way of testing the water. If you don't want to take your child there every day there is usually a coach pick-up from a point near your home.

Emily spent a week last summer at a Dolphin Camp where she learnt to paddle a canoe 'the length of two cars', took part in a video production, knocked down Coca Cola cans with a rifle, did gymnastics, BMX bikes, arts and crafts and umpteen other activities. Most day camps offer a non-stop programme of 'multi-activities' which means children get a chance to try a bit of everything, changing subject every hour or so. Instructors are 'trained', the ratio of children to staff is good and the idea is not just for the children to have fun but to improve existing skills and learn new ones. Even the little 'teenies', 3–5 year olds, on the Dolphin Camp had a go on the computers in between face-painting and trial bikes!

Sometimes a proportion of the children at the same camp will be 'boarders' so your children will be able to see for themselves what goes on if they stay next time. And there always seems to be a next time! Once a child goes to a summer centre, he's hooked.

Residential Camps

'Today was the most unforgetful day in my life.' (Emily, 8)

Residential camps are pretty similar to day camps, except that the activities go on until bedtime. The children often sleep in dormitories, are segregated into age-groups and sexes and thoroughly enjoy what for most of them is their first experience at being independent. Residential camps start at 5. If your child is apprehensive about going away on his own, see if you can fix it for a friend or relative to go at the same time.

You don't have to worry that your child will be bored or even miss you. He almost certainly won't have time. But don't make the mistake of choosing an unsuitable activity. There's no point in sending a child who hates the water on an intensive course on canoeing. Multi-activities are by far the best choice for first timers. Many camps specialise in a subject, like pony trekking or riding, sailing or canoeing. Or if your child is keen to improve a sport there are centres, often recognised by the relevant professional body, that provide intensive tuition.

Colony holidays are unique. They use less 'props' than the others and their basic philosophy is that children should learn to relate to each other through the activities. Shy children make new friends; hyperactive or bossy children suddenly learn to work together in a group; clingy children grow up overnight.

Wherever you choose to send your child you do have to be careful about safety. There are several questions you should get satisfactory answers to before you let your child go off and do potentially dangerous activities. The chapter in Part Two should ensure you find the best camp for your child.

Holidays for unaccompanied children aren't cheap. But if you could do with a bit of time to yourself during the long school holidays and you can afford it, try one. Neither you, nor your child, will regret it.

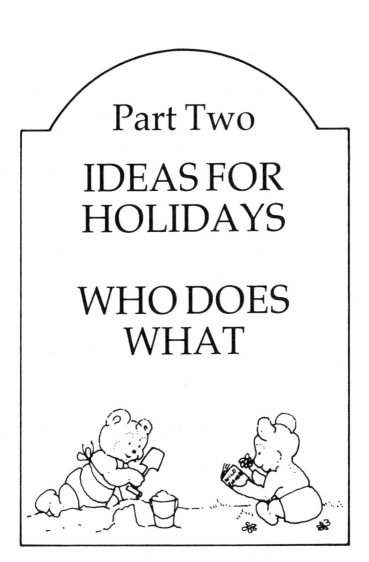

Part Two

IDEAS FOR HOLIDAYS

WHO DOES WHAT

In the following section I have singled out specific holiday ideas, broken down into different subjects and countries. It is by no means a comprehensive list of everything available for children. What I've done is selected operators who either have good reductions for families or offer holidays suitable for them. To get brochures either contact the tour operator direct (addresses at the back of the book) or go into a travel agent. To find out if there are any other tour operators to a particular place or attraction, contact the National Tourist Office of the country concerned.

I hope in sifting through my somewhat random list of suggestions, many of which are tried and tested, you'll come up with something you may not have thought about.

For future editions of this book I'd welcome any information on holidays you have personally experienced that you think could be included next time. Please fill in one of the forms at the end of the book. By the same token do feel free to let me know about any holiday specifically for families or children that you've tried and feel isn't all that it is made out to be.

9
COUNTRY BY COUNTRY

Every country in the world has its attractions for children. I can't hope to tell you about all of them here, what I can do is to round up a few specific holidays in various countries, some of them geared around attractions. It's a bit of a random selection, based on my travels, what's available in package tour brochures and suggestions from National Tourist Offices. You'll also find under each country heading a selection of other information you might find useful.

Contact the individual Tourist Boards for leaflets and brochures of specific attractions. If something particularly appeals, travel agents should be able to tell you about accommodation nearby and tour operators who go there. They will arrange independent travel if you need it.

I have only included countries you are likely to visit on a family holiday, most of them in Europe, a few, like the States and the Caribbean, outside it. Obviously there are many countries that I have left out but on the whole this was because they were either too far away or didn't have any specific attractions worth basing a whole holiday around.

First—Britain (England, Wales and Scotland), then Europe and further afield.

Britain

England

It would be impossible in this book to list everything there is for children to do and see in England and there's not enough space to describe each of the different regions. Suffice to say that the South West—Devon and Cornwall—are the most popular holiday destinations but that all the rest also have their fair share of attractions!

One of the good things about English holidays is that they are made up of a lot more than just the resort or place you happen to be in. Although the surrounding countryside is obviously important, so are a lot of other things, like the accommodation you are staying in (farm, holiday camp, rented cottage, seaside guesthouse), what's going on around you in the way of events and festivals and what there is to do and see.

All through the year, but particularly during the summer months, there are fairs and festivals happening all over England: festivals of music, carnivals, pageants, traditional events. There's absolutely nothing worse than arriving at your holiday destination to discover that you've missed an event by a day or two: it's a bit like getting to a party after the last guests have gone home! The English Tourist Board and regional offices (see pp. 196–7) publish lists of events—so you can find out what's happening before you fix your dates!

In other chapters I have covered quite a few different holiday ideas: holidaying at the seaside, farmhouse holidays, camping, activity and special interest holidays, self-catering, etc. Here are a few additional thoughts and a round-up of some of the biggest, newest and best attractions.

One of the best guidebooks to 'active' English holidays is the English Tourist Board's *Activity and Hobby Holidays* (from Tourist Information Centres and bookshops). It covers over 500 holidays throughout England that involve a particular hobby, interest or sport as an integral part of the package. Some are designed to demonstrate techniques and skills of various arts and crafts, others involve joining in to help you and your family improve your performance in a wide range of sports. There are quite a number of holidays described in the book specifically for families and also for unaccompanied children.

For general holiday ideas you can get a free brochure, *England Holidays*, on what to do, where to go and how to get there including details of inclusive holidays offered by tour operators. From travel agents or Tourist Information Centres.

Although there are hundreds of different attractions in England, from safari parks to castles, some of them are so exciting for children that you may think it worth arranging your holiday around a particular one.

New Attractions, Major Theme Parks and Revamped Old Favourites

Millions of pounds of money is being poured into leisure parks and new tourism projects all around Britain. A lot of the attractions are newly built, some have been there for years but have been given a thorough face-lift. Either way they all provide several days worth of fun. The following is a selection of new developments and revamped old-established favourites.

Alton Towers: combines formal gardens, historic buildings and 70 major attractions. Set in 800 acres. Rollercoaster and Black Hole space rides, reconstructed Victorian street, fairground, log flume, bobsleigh, copies of vintage cars to drive, doll museum. Alton, nr Ashbourne, North Staffordshire. Junction 16, M6. Tel: 0538 702449.

Camelot Theme Park: biggest in the North West. Based on Arthur and the Knights of the Round Table. Over 40 attractions including Merlin's cave, a circus, roller coaster, giant slide, aquatic world, train rides through the woods. One of the few theme parks where there is a hotel on site. Park Hall, Charnock Richard, Chorley, Preston, Lancs. Junction 27 or 28, M6. Tel: 0257 452090.

Bridlington: major indoor resort development due to open this year. You can also get aeroplane tours around the Bay and guided tours around the John Bull Rock Factory. Tel: 0262 78255.

Chessington Zoo: the old zoo is being revamped. Owned by Tussauds, millions of pounds is being invested to turn it into a 'World of Adventures'; they aim to make it the top family attraction in Britain. Due to open in 1987 (check before you go) visitors will be able to travel through the screen of a computer, career over the Rocky Mountains on a runaway train, sail around exotic lands of the Far East, and become part of a circus fantasy

Give them a funfair and you can take them anywhere.

world (non animal). Leatherhead Road, Chessington, Surrey. A243. Tel: 03727 27227.

Kinderland: Scarborough's fun, play and activity park is about getting back to basics, yet it is one of the most advanced children's adventure playgrounds in Europe. Girl Fridays provide general supervision. Lots for children and toddlers to do: boating lake, roller racers, log roll and water chute. Pay once for up to 10 hours of fun. Burniston Road, Scarborough, North Yorkshire. Tel: 0723 354555.

Lightwater Valley: Leisure Park with adventure playground, miniature railway, boating lake, Fort William centre. Pick your own fruit, visit the farm, model trains, toy museum, roller skate, canoe, mini motorbikes and a BMX track. North Stainley, nr Ripon, North Yorkshire. Tel: 0765 85321.

Pleasurewood Hills American Theme Park: East Anglia's first theme park in 50 acres of coastal countryside. Fairground-style entertainment in garden landscape, world of storybooks, roller skating, three-quarters of a mile long miniature railway. Western Town, vintage cars, paddle boats, pirate ship and BMX bikes. Corton, Lowestoft, Suffolk. Off A12. Tel: 0502 513626.

Sandcastle: Blackpool's £15 million indoor resort—the first in Europe: four pools, including wave pool with gently shelving beach, fun pool with floating island and harbour pool, waterslides, garden terraces, entertainment morning, noon and night, children's playland. 17 South Promenade, Blackpool (opposite Pleasure Beach). Tel: 0253 404013.

Solihull: Splashland at Tudor Grange claims to be the UK's first hydro-whip water slide. Being built while this book was going to press it is due to have three giant waterslides over 2,000 ft long, down which brave children and adults can zoom at speeds of up to 35 mph.

Thorpe Park: 500 acre theme park devoted to the history and achievements of maritime Britain. Lots of water-based attractions. Model World, historical aircraft, a Treasure Island train ride with pirates, Tea Cup Ride, farm with animals, watersports, children can roller skate around or take a pedalo. Summer jousting tournaments. Staines Road, Chertsey, Surrey. A320. Junction 2, M3. Tel: 09328 62633.

Wigan Pier: Winner of the British Tourist Authority's Travel Oscar, the Living Heritage centre was created out of a derelict canal and recreates the sights, sounds and smells of industrial Wigan in the year 1900. Street scenes with actors, lots to do and see including the world's largest working mill engine.

Wales

Wales and Scotland both have their own tourist boards (see p. 196) and regional offices. They produce excellent brochures on what to do and see, where to stay guides, guides to activity holidays, maps and lists of events. Here are a few thoughts that might set you off in the right direction.

Wales, where the sheep outnumber the people by about two to one, is conveniently compact for holiday touring, just 200 miles from north to south and it is easy to get around.

North Wales has been attracting visitors since Victorian times. Around Snowdon, the highest peak in England and Wales, there are miles of nature trails, dissected by rivers and waterfalls. On the north coast are seaside resorts like big brash Rhyl, Colwyn Bay and the still dignified resort of Llandudno.

In the West are the usually quiet beaches of the Lleyn Peninsula, the sweeping sand dunes of Cardigan Bay, the genuinely un-spoilt coastline of Pembrokeshire and seasides like Tenby, with its gaily painted houses.

Mid Wales is often overlooked but if offers an excellent alterna-tive to the coast: the red sandstone heights of the Brecon Beacons are ideal for walking, you can pony trek in the Black Mountains, or fish for salmon or trout in one of the numerous rivers. Each year they hold a Festival of the Countryside (June to September), set in 3,000 square miles of it: 400 activities are offered from walks and water pursuits to archaeology and gold panning.

The best of the South is the Gower Peninsula, designated an area of outstanding natural beauty, with splendid cliffs and some good beaches.

Wherever you travel you'll see plenty of evidence of the bloody border struggles between England and Wales, particu-larly along Offa's Dyke, the wall built by King Offa in the eighth century to defend England against marauding Welshmen. There are plenty of castles to explore, like Conwy, Caernarfon and Caerphilly. The possibilities for children are endless: you can take them for a trip down a coal mine, on a ride on one of the great little trains of Wales, to visit a working woollen mill, canoeing, riding, sailing, or to Rhyl's Sun Centre, three lagoon-style swimming pools with surfing and a Welsh Dragon slide all under one roof.

Pony trekking is one of the most popular holidays in Wales, and most centres welcome beginners. The Wales Tourist Board will send you a booklet of those that meet the standards laid down by the Pony Trekking and Riding Society of Wales.

Farmhouse holidays are well-established in Wales (listed in the *Where to Stay in Wales* guide).

Activity holidays: PGL have multi-choice activity holidays for families, and for unaccompanied children, in centres in North Wales, the Wye Valley (Monmouth School for Girls) and the Brecon Beacons (caravans) where you can do a range of activities or specialise in sailing, windsurfing, riding or pony trekking. HF holidays have family walking holidays at their centres in Conwy specially geared to little legs (there are even walkers with pushchairs). Babies can be left in a crèche, under 5's go free and there are good reductions on rail travel.

Self-catering in cottages, bungalows and farms as well as in caravan parks is also very popular. You can get Golden Rail packages that save on travel costs. Every property is inspected by the Wales Tourist Board—and if you want them, groceries can be delivered to await your arrival. Standards of accommodation at caravan parks are high and the Welsh Dragon Award is given to particular caravan parks that reach an exacting criteria.
Several of the large holiday centres have caravan and chalet sites in Wales (Haven and Pontin's among them). Butlin's have two holiday centres with a non-stop programme of activities, one at Barry Island, the other at Pwllheli in North Wales where the miniature railway will take you to the beach. And Ladbroke have a centre at Carmarthen Bay.

SuperTed was born in Wales, and SuperTed weekends (October to May), for families with young children, are held in the middle of Wales at Llandrindod Wells. The cartoon character and his friends take children on local outings and play with them at the Metropole Hotel, while parents get on with other things. Great fun for under 7's. Tel: 0597 2600.

Scotland

There's a lot more to Scotland than bagpipes, tartans, haggis and whisky. The scenery is splendid from the rugged indented west coast and the islands of Mull and Skye to the heather-covered moors, high mountains and deep lochs of the central Highlands. You can always go on a Nessie spotting expedition! The Borders were the scene of many a battle and the area is thick with castles and abbeys all of which are used to being clambered over by children. Edinburgh has plenty of interest, especially at Festival time. You can visit the Highlands when the Games or sheep dog trials are going on or Aberdeen when the World Pipe Band Championships are held in August.
The Scottish Tourist Board produces a number of useful publications, including: *Adventure and Special Interest Holidays in Scotland*; *Scottish Farmhouse Holidays (Highlands and Islands)*; and a free brochure called *Holiday Scotland* which has

a section devoted to families and hotels that cater for them, allowing under 16's to share your room for free. If you book one of these inclusive holidays you get a National Trust for Scotland pass which will let you into 95 castles, stately homes, battlefields and gardens for nothing.

Riding holidays: The Scottish Trekking and Riding Association has a leaflet on centres with holiday facilities. Pony trekking with sure-footed Highland ponies originated in Scotland and this sort of holiday is totally suitable for beginners.

Family walking holidays are offered at HF centres at Loch Awe and Loch Leven.

Activity holidays: PGL Family Adventure Holidays are based at the University of Stirling and offer multi-activities as well as riding. The Scottish Youth Hostels Association run Breakaway Holidays: trail riding in the Trossachs, climbing in Glencoe, pony trekking in the Borders, as well as walking and caving, canoeing, cycle tours and skiing both cross country and down-hill in Glenshee and the Cairngorms. Some centres run specific holidays for unaccompanied children.

Butlin's have a centre at Ayr. Indoor and outdoor pool with free lessons for children. Children's entertainment. BATS scheme for active teenagers who want to try out new sports and activities. Night Owl service where babies up to 9 months can be left in the care of qualified children's nurses and nappies can be washed too! Accommodation in five star caravans and flats.

Europe and Further Afield

Austria

Austria is very good at looking after visitors' children. The National Tourist Office produces a large number of useful brochures, split up into the different regions (there are 77 of them), including holidays on farms. In winter lots of resorts run ski kindergartens; English is spoken and you can leave children from 3 upwards. There is a weekly charge for ski instruction, supervision and food, and it is best to book in advance. Several tour operators have all-inclusive packages to ski resorts with kindergartens (see skiing, p. 80). The Children's Wonderland at Vorarlberg—a tiny area between Lake Constance and the Rhine —covers over 40 resorts. Most run kindergartens, outings, tennis camps (10–16's), forest trails, computer camps, mountain adventures, sports instruction and fun and games for younger children. English-speaking supervision. Hotels and guesthouses are geared up for families and the children join up daily for the activities. Details from the National Tourist Office.

Balearics

Majorca, Ibiza, Minorca have been tried and tested for well over a decade. There are numerous hotels on all the islands that cater well for children (see Sol Hotels, p. 89) and some good, if crowded beaches (the best are on Minorca). The larger tour operators run supervised miniclubs during the day. Lancaster Family First have hotels with Mothercare playrooms and equipment, plus all sorts of facilities for young families (see p. 88).

Caribbean

There's absolutely no reason why you shouldn't venture this far (apart from cost). Children don't seem to suffer unduly from jetlag, school-age children will have had the right jabs and the food is generally Americanised, with plenty of fresh fruit and local fish to eat as well as hamburgers and chips. Some hotels will provide cots and highchairs. Since meals are expensive, check if there are reductions for children. Obviously the sun is going to be hot so keep them out of it at midday, and take plenty of insect repellent.

Caribbean. No reason why you shouldn't venture this far.

Packages and hotels: Tradewinds and Kuoni both make excellent offers to one under-12-year-old prepared to share your room. Tradewinds offer free holidays to Barbados and St Lucia and charge a nominal amount for Grenada (Caribbean Airways) in March, May, June, October and November or for a flat fare of £125 to Antigua, St Lucia and Barbados (British Airways) from January to June, and September to November. Food is payable on the spot (and isn't cheap). Kuoni charge a flat £99 to Barbados, Antigua and St Lucia (and include meals at one hotel), all year except mid to end of December, mid to end April, and from 7 July to end September.

On St Lucia one of the best hotels for families is the St Lucian (I can personally vouch for it). The hotel is right on a gently shelving beach, there is a playground, swimming pool (but no separate paddling pool), children's hostesses, activities, and children's menus. The vegetation is tropical jungle, quite educational: plantations of bananas, cocoa, coffee, etc. No more hazardous healthwise than travelling to Europe.

Club Méditerranée have miniclubs for children at Eleuthera (2−11's) and Paradise Island (from 4 months) on the Bahamas. Both also have Circus Schools where children can safely learn to swing on the trapezes, juggle and do all sorts of circus acts. Grand show of talent at the end. Club Med. go to other Caribbean destinations too but although the Clubs will take children over 6 there are no special facilities.

On Jamaica, the Wyndham Rose Hall Beach Hotel and Country Club on Montego Bay's long sandy beach has a Kids Korner with supervised activities for over 3's from 9 until noon and 2−5. Children under 18 stay free with an adult. Championship golf course, floodlit tennis, sailing, parasailing, waterskiing, etc. Book direct (contact the Tourist Board).

Denmark

Denmark offers a lot for families and most Danes speak English.

Farmhouse holidays are very popular with English families who mostly travel by ship with their own car. You eat with the family and can even match your children's ages with those of the farmer's (see farms, p. 102).

Self-catering is also popular in holiday complexes on the somewhat exposed west coast of Jutland (good sandy beaches that go out for miles at low tide), or in summerhouses all over Denmark, including on Funen, a quiet, rural island, home of Hans Christian Andersen.

Legoland: By far the most popular Danish attraction is Legoland in the middle of Jutland:

Legoland: built out of 30 million bits of Lego (Denmark).

'I cannot say a word which will match how brilliant it is, it is wonderful, amazing, brilliant, spectacular, fantastic and great ten times over.' (Annie, 6)

50 years ago a Danish carpenter decided to make bricks for children out of plastic. Today Legoland, in Billund (built out of 30 million of them), is Denmark's most famous attraction after the Tivoli Gardens in Copenhagen. Almost half the visitors to Denmark from Britain go specifically to visit it. It is right in the middle of Jutland (45 mins drive from the port of Esbjerg, next to tiny Billund airport; Maersk Air fly you right there from Southend). Appeals to children up to about 12 with full-scale models (Fabuland and Lego), plus rides (safari park, through a gold mine, river boat, monorail), junior driving school, indoor Lego-building competitions, toy and doll exhibitions, emphasis on family fun. Although the surrounding countryside is very pleasant (woodland and fjords) there's not a lot for parents to do. Packages often include the entrance fee but it isn't expensive and you can get cards that allow children eight rides for a fixed price. Pushchairs are available. Cafés and restaurants sell snacks, meals and ice-cream, but no sweets! A long weekend is probably long enough.

Copenhagen: Tivoli Gardens has rides and shows, summer fireworks and concerts; also nearby Bakken in beechwoods has puppetshows, and along the coast north of Copenhagen you can explore Hamlet's Castle, at Elsinore.

Packages to all the above with Scanscape (Scanhomes), or DFDS Longship Holidays. Contact the Danish Tourist Board who produce booklets on farmhouse holidays and a special HEI booklet for children.

France

A good choice if your children have started to learn French at school. Lots of possibilities by ship with your own car. Also family trains with specially converted carriages for young children to play in.

Gîtes: Possibly the most suitable holidays in France with children are *gîte*-based (see farms). *Gîtes* are converted farm buildings, in rural areas, often in small villages where you quickly become part of local life. Most are self-catering (although you can get dinner) and inland. A large number are on working farms. Perhaps more suitable if you are taking a few children as one might get bored.

Book direct through the Gîtes de France (send sae for details), 178 Piccadilly, London W1. All-inclusive packages with Brittany Ferries, Townsend Thoresen, Sealink and Sally Line.

Skiing: The French Government Tourist Office publish a booklet called *Ski France* which lists resorts with day nurseries. Lots of tour operators package up ski holidays. Club Méditerranée have skiing villages at Pompadour, Alpe d'Huez, Les Arcs, Avoriaz and Chamonix (miniclubs from 4 years), and at Tignes val Claret (miniclub from 6 years). Summer Clubs at Vittel (baby club from 4 months, miniclub from 4 years, and kids club from 8 years). There is also a Club Méditerranée at Cargese in Corsica (miniclub and kids club).

Paris: Suitable for older children. Take them up the Eiffel Tower, along the Seine on a Bâteau Mouche (most of the sites are visible from the river) and at weekends to the Beaubourg (a bit like our Covent Garden). Numerous tour operators, ask travel agents.

Germany

The Brothers Grimm are Germany's main draw for children. Responsible for Puss in Boots and the Golden Goose, the dwarfs, fairies and mermaids are still around, as they were in the early nineteenth century when Jacob and Wilhelm Grimm told their stories. These days you can follow the Fairy Tale Road, from their birthplace at Hanau on the Main, through Bremen and along the River Main to the coast. On the way you'll see Sleeping Beauty's castle (surrounded these days not only by a primeval forest but a wildlife park), the hills where Snow White took refuge with the Seven Dwarfs, you can visit the land of Hansel and Gretel and watch fairy tales performed in puppet theatres and in the open air. The German Tourist Board produce a fairy tale route map, with places of interest for grown ups too.

Take your own car with DFDS and then follow your own itinerary. DER have packages to some of the places *en route*.

Phantasialand: If you are driving in Germany and happen to be near the Autobahn 553, south of Koln, turn off onto the B51 for Phantasialand, 'Europe's biggest leisure and adventure paradise' (packed with rides). Open from April to the end of October.

By coach, DFDS Longship Holidays have a 5 night combined tour of Legoland in Denmark and Hansaland in Northern Germany (leisure park with endless amusements: dolphinarium, water rides, Wild West Town, etc.).

Greece

Most of the larger tour operators and several specialists offer holidays to the mainland and islands. Several run supervised miniclubs for children in Greek hotels (particularly on the larger islands). If you are planning to go to smaller islands that don't have airports, travelling time can be lengthy and involve long boat trips. Under 6's get discounts on ferries. Good beaches in the Halkidiki on the mainland. Older children may enjoy the various sites and museums in Athens.

Packages: Olympic Holidays have Robinson Clubs (a sort of Club Med. concept, originally conceived for Germans) in Corfu, Crete and Zante, and at Nea Sivota and Halkidiki on the mainland. There are trained instructors in a wide range of sports, and prices are all-inclusive including all meals and wine (you pay for drinks with beads). Supervised activities for children (from 4 or 6 upwards depending on resort). Other holidays with Sunmed, Thomson and most major tour operators.

Holland

The Netherlands Board of Tourism has a leaflet of all children's attractions in Holland including Holland's own version of Legoland, Madurodam in the Hague; a miniature Dutch community in action; the famous cheese markets at Gouda and Alkmaar. There are also numerous windmills, you can see clogs being carved, visit the costumed villages of Marken and Volendam, and the biggest flower auction in the world at Aalsmeer. At the Witches Weighing Stool of Oudewater (near Utrecht) they used to weigh people accused of witchcraft, thousands flocked there in the seventeenth to nineteenth centuries for proof of their innocence—a certificate stating they were too heavy to travel by broomstick. Kids can have themselves weighed on the original scales.

Look for tourist menus in restaurants, good savings and children's menus. If you plan sightseeing, buy a museum card; under 25's can get in free.

Flat, so take your bikes or hire from Netherlands Railways.

Children's hotel: The Hans Brinker House, by the sea. Children between 3 and 12 are accepted in summer (babies from 3 weeks during winter). It is run by two registered nurses and you can leave them in safe hands while you go off for the day (Erasmus-weg 3, Noordwick aan Zee. Tel: 01719 2753).

Self-catering: Holland's 5★ Center Parcs are excellent for families. Accommodation is in bungalows, and there are several in different locations. Children's playschools (3—12's) with professional supervisors, organised activities, cyclecross race tracks, subtropical swimming paradise and babysitting. Lots for adults too including an artificial ski-slope, sauna, cycling, bowling, tennis, jogging track, surfing. Butchers, off-licence and supermarkets on site as well as restaurants. Bungalows come with playpens, highchairs and campbeds.

Through Thomas Cook Holiday Shops or Sealink.

Ireland

Children are welcomed enthusiastically in Ireland. There are no quarantine laws so you can even take the cat.

Sealink and B&I have free offers for under 16's in mobile homes and caravans. Also Aer Lingus and CIE Tours.

The Irish Tourist Board produce a *Discover Young Ireland* brochure which includes summer schools, working holidays, activity and sports holidays. If you are taking a car through County Cork, don't miss the Fota Wildlife Park (where they breed endangered species).

Packages to self-catering properties and farms (see p. 102), also cruising on the River Shannon—slow but good fun for children. Or how about a leisurely horse-drawn caravan holiday; they sleep four comfortably. CIE Tours have them in County Wicklow.

Israel

Eilat in southern Israel is a good winter sun destination. A bit too hot to take children to in summer (average 86°F), the coldest month is January when the maximum temperature is 70°F. Club In is a Ladbroke-owned self-catering villa resort and is across the road from a sandy beach about 4½ miles from Eilat town. Good sports facilities, some of the best diving in the world, windsurfing, snorkelling, waterskiing and Coral World, an underwater observatory where you can see the fish without getting wet. Floodlit tennis, pool, plus paddling pool, and special play area for children with organised indoor and outdoor activities in the Kids Corner Club throughout the day. Nightclub and baby listening, launderette, supermarket. Camel, jeep or horse rides into the desert. Club Méditerranée village at Coral Beach with a miniclub for over 4's.

Packages: Wings/OSL, El Al Superstar, Peltours, Club Méditerranée, Speedwing.

Kibbutz Inns (three star hotels) and Kibbutz Holiday Villages (chalets and apartments) make interesting bases all over Israel, from the shores of the Dead Sea to the hills of the Galilee. Most kibbutzim are agricultural with everything produced, earned and shared by the whole community. You'll get fresh farm food, some have pools, all have good facilities and babysitting. The *Israel Tourist Hotels* booklet (from the Israel Government Tourist Office) lists addresses; fly-drive packages with Peltours.

Italy

Italians love children and wherever you go your family will be enthusiastically welcomed. Bear in mind that southern Italy (and Sardinia and Sicily) can get very hot indeed in August. There are numerous family seasides on both coastlines of Italy and on the islands of Sicily and Sardinia. Some of the best and safest beaches for children in Europe are along the Adriatic; Rimini and Lido di Jesolo have miles of soft sandy beaches that shelve gently into the sea, backed almost continuously by hotels (but less high rise than Spain) and campsites. Most Italian seasides have a lot more character than Spanish ones and places of interest are nearby. From Lido di Jesolo you can get to Venice, or Padua; from Rimini, the tiny State of San Marino; from Viareggio, Pisa and Tuscany.

Santa Maria di Castellabate: In southern Italy the tiny old-fashioned seaside resort of Santa Maria di Castellabate is ideal if you're taking young children. If you like a peaceful sort of place this is it, though it does run to several bars and restaurants, and a good main street for shopping. Miles of unspoilt countryside all around (mountains, olive groves, rugged coastline, orchards and ruined sites to visit: Paestum, Pompei and Velia). Book through Magic of Italy, CV Travel.

Planet Maratea: About 140 miles south of Naples in Basilicata, the modern Planet Maratea is a large holiday complex, just over a mile above the sea. It is in a fairly isolated spot with views of mountains and volcanic beaches below (free shuttle). The complex has Olympic-sized pools, kids paddling pool, tennis, piano bar, classes in yoga and keep fit, plus a playground and hostesses who arrange activities during the day. Baby listening. **Packages**: Citalia.

The Islands: Sardinia: The well-established Forte Village in pine woods in the south is vast, with a good beach, several restaurants and bars, tennis, swimming pools, aerobic classes, bikes to hire, and a long list of sports facilities. All day nursery for babies (pay there), a children's centre which is constantly supervised, adventure playground, trampolining, own clubhouse for teenagers. Babysitting. Also self-catering cottages. **Packages**: Citalia.

Sicily is the largest island in the Mediterranean, the best resort for families is Cefalu in the north; lovely soft sand beach with the old, very picturesque town to one side of it.

Book through Magic of Italy, and Citalia, Hotels and Apartments.

Club Méditerranée have villages at Kamarina on Sicily (miniclub from 2 years, Circus School from 4). On the mainland, in winter, there is the ski resort of Sestriere (miniclub from 4 years). Club Valtur (similar to Club Med.) concentrates its villages with facilities for children in the south, although there is also one for older children in the mountains of Piedmont in the north.

Norway

Like the rest of Scandinavia there's plenty of interest for children and a sympathetic price structure on transport, and in hotels and restaurants. Look for the bear symbol with the word Feriemeny to find restaurants serving a special children's platter. If you are touring with your own car and arrive by ship you can use the Scandinavian Bonus Pass to get reductions in hotels (children under 15 get free bed and breakfast). Holiday possibilities include self-catering in wooden chalets with grass growing on the roofs, numerous activity holidays, especially around the fjords. The Gloppen adventure sounds good if you've got older children: canoeing, mountaineering, windsurfing and trekking safaris into the land of trolls. Or you can stay in the family youth hostels at Balestrand, ride Iceland ponies, sail or canoe. If you are touring, stop off at the Lekeland playland in Skien, the Telemark Summerland at Bo (both in the Telemark region) and don't miss the Children's Museum in Oslo. If you arrive by ship at Stavanger, the Kongeparken theme

Rent a bike with a baby seat.

park, the largest recreation centre in Norway, is 17 miles south at Algard. Bobsleigh run over 3,000 ft long, Lilliput traffic school, lakes, and fairy tale people. Focal point is a 260 ft long prostrate Gulliver—you enter him through his ears, his hair is a climbing frame, the picnic area is in his right hand, and there's a lookout in his nostrils! Hotel and camping on site. Wherever you go you can hire bikes, often with babyseats on the back.
Packages: NSR Travel Bureau, Norway Line, Fred Olsen Lines.

Portugal

The Algarve is the area most suitable for family holidays with over 150 miles of sandy beaches. You can get yourself a fair bit if privacy as there are many small rocky coves (attractive rock formations on the sand). Access is often down steep steps from the clifftop hotels and villas. Atlantic seas can get rough and may be still chilly at Easter. Mild climate in winter. Lots of wild flowers and greenery and not nearly as built up as the Spanish Costas. Several aparthotels, flats, villas, small pensions and large luxury hotels with their own golf courses, tennis courts, etc. Discos, nightclubs and casinos in the bigger resorts; peace and quiet outside them.
Packages: A large number of tour operators (ask your travel agent). Also (direct-sell) Travel Club of Upminster specialise in the area and have very good reductions for children and teenagers (up to 19).

Spain

Best holidays for families are with Sol Hotels, see accommodation, p. 89. Most of the major tour operators feature Sol Hotels in their holiday brochures.

La Manga Club: 60 miles south of Alicante, a large estate combining leisure, sports and social facilities (including two championship golf courses, 18 tennis courts, riding), three pools, restaurants, bars and discos. Villa, hotel or apartment accommodation. Miniclub in the school holidays for 2–17's. Children can spend the day there and eat all together. Lots of activities: treasure hunts, mini disco, riding, watersports, etc.
Packages: Sovereign (golf programme), Arrow, Peter Stuyvesant Travel. Also Club Méditerranée (winter and summer) village at Don Miguel, Marbella with baby club (4 months) and miniclub (from 4 years).

Sweden

Sweden has lots of theme parks and zoos, several claiming to the biggest of their kind in Europe! Including:
Sommarland, in Vastergotland at Skara, a few hours drive from Gothenburg (the largest aqua park in Europe), with giant fairy tale pools (you can camp there);
Kolmarden (the largest zoo in Europe), safari park, dolphin

shows, waxworks, Europe's longest cableway, hotel, camping and caravan site; and

Liseberg in south Gothenburg (under 6's free, the largest funfair in Europe) with circus school, entertainment, rides (the hotel Liseberg Heden is five minutes away with free entry to the park).

SantaWorld is about 9 miles south of Mora (3 hours drive from Stockholm). Santa lives there with his reindeers, the Snow-queen, a living snowman called Dusty and fairy tale characters. Children can visit his toy factory, take part in activities, and see books in his house where the names of all children are written down with a record of their Christmas presents. Open all year, more realistic in winter in the snow. Also in the vicinity a bear park and the wooden horse factory.

Stockholm's attractions include Skansen, an outdoor museum, and Grona Land amusement park. If you are planning visits to museums and fun parks, ask the tourist board about the special card you can buy giving free entry.

Packages: Sweden also offers a wide range of self-catering possibilities, from isolated log cabins with grass growing on the roofs to holiday villages with good facilities. DFDS (by ship), take your own car. Or Norwegian State Railways.

Switzerland

The Swiss National Tourist Office has a large number of book-lets and leaflets on family holidays (hotels, free transport cards, kindergartens at ski resorts). There is also a comprehensive booklet called *Holidays in Switzerland for Young People* that covers everything from camping and farms to sports, hobby holidays or staying as a guest with a Swiss family.

Saas Fee: Summer skiing resort with tennis, Leisure Centre, guided walks, handicraft courses (glass engraving, carving, etc.), with youth camps (8–16) in tennis and skiing. Book through Kuoni, Swiss Travel Service.

Lenzerheide, on top of a mountain pass, in pine forests above a lake, is a resort that caters particularly well for children. Super-vised activities two to four times a week (8am to 5pm) and optional sports programme for adults. Also excursions (learn to make cheese, etc.). Book through Kuoni (with special deals for children).

Skiing: Club Med. has several villages where children can learn to ski and also be left to get on with other activities in the miniclubs (from 4 years). Resorts: Engelberg, Leysin Belvedere (from 4 months), Pontresina, St Moritz Roi Soleil, St Moritz Victoria, Valbella, Villars, Wengen and Zinal (from 4 months).

Disneyland, every child's dream holiday (USA).

United States

Disney

'The best thing was the Journey into Imagination—we saw a dream catching machine and at the end of it was a dragon.' (David, 9)

'In Tomorrow Land you saw lettuces growing in space!' (Paul, 8)

'We had breakfast with all the Disney characters on a paddle steamer.' (Sophie, 4)

Florida has to rank as favourite for a holiday destination. It is magic land, a children's paradise of theme parks: Walt Disney World, the futuristic Epcot Centre, Kennedy Space Centre, Sea World and Planet Ocean among them. Although you might think it is too far to take young children, most seem unaffected by the journey or the time change. Fortunately for parents there is more to Florida than Disney and plenty of good beaches to relax on.

'In the sea were sting rays and sharks but that did not stop us going in.' (Nicola, 6)

Packages: Under 12's qualify for the best deals to Florida depending on when you travel. Jetsave extend discounts to under 18's. Some tour operators include all sorts of extras from free entrance to the theme parks to free breakfasts at hotels (not restricted to under 12's), even car hire. American Express Holidays use Magic Kingdom hotels inside Walt Disney World itself so you don't have to move at all! Other hotels worth considering include: the new Hilton at Walt Disney World which has a Youth Hotel with supervised activities for 3–12's from 9 in the morning until late at night, and free transport to the Magic Kingdom and Epcot. Children stay free sharing their parents' room as they do at a large number of hotels in the States. The Wyndham across the road from Sea World has a supervised playroom for guests with cots, games, entertainer (2pm–7pm), plus for all the family magicians, music etc. in the vast lobby, which has waterfalls and an aviary. Holiday Inn Main Gate East has a daily free 'Only for Kids' programme—they eat in the 'Gingerbread House'. Holiday Hound Clubhouse, puppet shows, games, playground, kids pool and Olympic pool for adults.

About 40 minutes from Orlando the Village of Grenelefe is a 1,000 acre sports complex where children under 18 stay free if they share their parents' apartment. Top quality sports facilities include: tennis, swimming, three championship golf courses and daylong supervised activities for children.

California: Anaheim is the home of the original Disneyland, now in its fourth decade. It gets bigger by the year. Also nearby: Knott's Berry Farm; five theme parks and home of Snoopy and Charlie Brown; Marineland and Sea World with the world's largest shark exhibit; and behind the scenes tours of NBC and Universal Studios.
Packages: American Express, Poundstretcher, Virgin and Jetsave. (Check car hire arrangements, tour operators may include it free or for a nominal amount.)

Other USA possibilities

Club Med. have A Kids of the World summer camp based at Copper Mountain in Colorado. The village has a miniclub for over 3's but the summer camp is a separate thing and children from 8 upwards go on their own. Usual range of sports activities plus Circus School, computer labs, whitewater rafting, jeep rides and train journeys through the gold-mining country of the Wild West. One leader to every six children, divided up into groups: 8 and 9's, 10 and 11's, 12 and 13's. Not cheap. Kids usually go for a month. Escorted travel from the UK. Also in the States, Club Med. Sandpiper village in Florida (miniclub from 2 years, kids club from 8), bungalows along the river St Lucie.

Ranch Holidays: Got a kid with Wild West fantasies? Fancy rounding up the cattle on a dude ranch in Arizona, Wyoming or Montana? Spend your days riding out with working cowboys as if you were a real cowpoke, learn to rope a calf, eat round a campfire, sleep under canvas, canoe, ride the rapids and explore the trails ridden by Indians, prospectors and settlers.

American Round-Up (with Northwest Orient) have packages, fly-drive, to a large selection of ranches all over the States, some small and homely, others with golf courses, pools, jacuzzis, tennis pros, etc. Many suitable for families with 'full-time counsellors supervising children's programmes'. A few under canvas, although most aren't and have twentieth century comforts.

Yugoslavia

Club Méditerranée have villages at Pakostane (clubs for 2's upwards) and Sveti Marki (from 8 upwards). Several suitable hotels in the Yugotours brochure. Best holiday complex for children is the Plava Laguna in Porec, which has supervised children's clubs. Best beaches are in Montenegro, around Ulcinj.

10
PACKAGE
TOURS

On a straightforward beach holiday children can get *bored*! In fact they can drive you crazy. One of the best ways to ensure that you don't have to spend your entire time on your hands and knees making sandcastles or in desperation let them go off on their own and then worry about what they are getting up to, is to choose a holiday that provides supervision and activities on the spot.

Miniclubs

'There was this little hut round the pool and you could draw and do what you like and they gave you a drink and some fruit, it gives you something to do apart from swimming.' (Ann, 9)

There are an increasing number of tour operators who run miniclubs at several of the resorts or hotels in their brochures. The clubs are usually for the exclusive use of their clients and are divided into different age-groups. They are usually run by trained nursery nurses and teachers, simply because most tour operators are inundated with qualified applicants.

In practice, what you get varies considerably between tour operators and individual hotels. It also depends on how many children there are at the resort in any given week. The special children's clubs may not run if there aren't enough of them. Brochures are often deliberately vague about what you should expect. It ranges from a couple of hours of supervised fun and games on the beach to daylong activities and outings. Check beforehand if the number of hours of freedom you get, or the number of hours of entertainment the children get, depending on which way you look at it, is important to you. Many of the 'clubs' only operate in the mornings for a couple of hours and offer little except supervised play. They aren't really stimulating enough for older children. On the other hand some holiday club operators (like Club Med. and HCI) have a virtually non-stop programme of entertainment and activities guaranteed to amuse even the most restless of children (see p. 116). Some will also teach them various sporting activities, although you should check that instructors are properly qualified, that there are enough of them for the number of children, and that they speak your language.

The larger tour operators offer children all sorts of other perks too from T-shirts to puzzle books, competitions, outings, communal bedtime stories, beach balls, and follow-up Christmas and birthday cards!

Sometimes it is the hotel itself rather than the tour operator who provides the fun and games. Many large tour operators use the Sol Hotel chain in Spain. Their hotels are on the Costas and on the islands and they cater exceptionally well for children, with children's clubs, good reductions plus genuine free places and generous discounts for single parents. The hotels feature in most of the large tour operators' programmes.

For holidays geared around specific activities, rather than ordinary holidays with activities thrown in, see the chapter on activity holidays (p. 119).

A brief mention here of holiday camps, villages, centres and clubs, because they are also sold as package tours (for full details, see pp. 112–18). Club Méditerranée (who aren't cheap) win my award for the best supervision and tuition and for taking children from 4 months and upwards off your hands from 9 in the morning until 9 at night. Club Valtur offer a similar arrangement in southern Italy, and HCI will also take children over 5 off your hands from early morning until 9 at night, but the children have to eat with you. The difference between going to one of these villages and using a miniclub with an ordinary tour operator is that your children will mix with children from other nationalities (children quickly learn to communicate even if they have no common language). The other advantage (or otherwise) is that there are activities going on for parents as well as children.

Tour Operators with Supervised Activities, Special Hotels or Facilities for Children

Cosmos: OK Club. Certain resorts and hotels. 2–12. Six days a week. Supervised games, gifts, communal bedtime stories, and follow up birthday cards. Hours vary from hotel to hotel. Kiddie Patrol.

Falcon Family Holidays: Club 10 and Trouble Club (4–11's). Five days a week, morning and afternoon with games, treasure hunts. Trouble Club supervised nursery for under 4's, minimum one hour a day, five days a week. Buggy hire. Room patrols. Reductions up to 16's on apartment holidays. Good offers for families of four.

Global: Wizzy Club. 3–12. Selected apartments. Six days a week. Wizzy patrol.

Horizon: Hippo Club. 3–11. Six days. Selection of hotels. Many of the children's reps are trained nursery nurses. Games, competitions, parties, bedtime stories, supervised early meals. Baby Patrol.

Intasun: Carefree Kids Club. 3–12. Wide selection of resorts and hotels. 5, 6 or 7 days. Supervisors have previous experience of working with children (nannies, junior school teachers), games, sports, rambles, bedtime stories. Kiddie Patrol.

Lancaster Family First: First Mates Club for 3–12's at hotels/apartments. English-speaking trained supervisors. Six days a week, minimum three hours a day. Usual range of activities and competitions, outings, mini discos, bedtime stories. Early suppers. Baby patrolling. Good reductions for children (up to 16 in some cases and for single parents outside peak season). Mothercare-equipped Mother and Baby Rooms in selected hotels (Spanish mainland and Majorca, one each in Italy and Portugal).

Sunmed: Sunbeam Clubs on a handful of Greek islands and on mainland Greece in summer and a Snowflake Club at ski resorts (centrally heated nursery) in winter. Run by qualified English nursery nurses. Six hours a day, six days a week, dependent on ages and numbers of children.

Thomson: The first tour operator to introduce a special service for children. Big T Clubs, for 3–11's at a large number of hotels. The clubs are headed by Tommy Seagull, and run 'nearly always' by trained nursery nurses and teachers. Games, activities and special excursions, competitions, birthday cards. Minimum three hours a day, six days a week. Bedtime stories. Baby patrolling.

Tjaereborg: Tjaerebear Club, 3–10, three hours a day, six days a week. Nominal charge then all activities free. There will be Scandinavian children at some resorts. Childminding.

Most of the tour operators who offer special programmes for children usually also offer good discounts, early mealtimes, cots, highchairs and babysitting.

11

BEACHES

I can't give you a guide to all the best beaches in Britain or abroad here, there are too many. All I can tell you is that the best ones for children have soft sand that shelves gently into the sea; plenty of shade; no tar, seaweed, pebbles or pollution; have nearby loos; and a café or restaurant. And that no beach is safe, there are just some that are safer than others. However beautiful a beach might look in a holiday brochure, you can't usually tell from the photos just how suitable it is going to be for children.

Hazards

One of the hazards is, of course, pollution, in the UK as well as abroad. Sewage is unpleasant rather than dangerous. Recent studies show that you face a slightly higher risk of mild stomach upsets if you swim in water polluted by sewage. You shouldn't swim in dirty sea and you should avoid sitting near a sewage outlet. Wherever you are try and ensure your children keep their mouths closed when swimming! Assume that anything coming out of a pipe in the sand is polluted and don't let the children paddle in it. Avoid any beach that looks visibly polluted. The EEC have recommended limits of sewage pollution and a legal maximum, yet there have been serious problems over past years (now under control) in Portugal and on beaches in Britain. Wherever you go in Southern Europe do not drink the tap water.

Rough seas are, of course, dangerous. Many of the larger beach resorts in Europe operate a flag warning system. How reliable it is varies from resort to resort. It may be only in operation during the peak summer months so if you don't see a flag don't assume that swimming is safe. Generally a red flag means bathing is forbidden, a yellow flag means that you are allowed in but swimming is dangerous and a green flag denotes the all clear. You may see a chequered flag, which could mean that although there is usually a lifeguard in attendance, while it is flying, he's otherwise engaged.

To avoid little feet being cut by rocks or treading on sea urchins it may be an idea to invest in a pair of plastic shoes. Pack some oil of Eucalyptus for removing tar, a sun umbrella if there isn't going to be any shade and a thermos for taking drinks with you. Also see Health (p. 165) for beaches abroad where there is a risk of picking up creeping eruption, a worm that can enter the skin through bare feet.

How to Find a Good Beach

On the whole, tour operators do their best to direct parents with small children towards resorts with safe and sandy beaches. Often they have a special symbol in their holiday brochures. What they often don't say though, is whether the sand is soft or grainy, how hot it gets underfoot at midday, how much natural shade there is, whether there is seaweed or pebbles in the sea, tar or litter on the sand, where the nearest Coke and ice-lolly shop, loo or showers are or just how crowded it is going to get during July and August. Plus, most important of all, if you've got toddlers or young children, how steeply it shelves into the sea. Usually it is pretty hard to find out everything about a beach until you get there.

Wherever you go check just how far from the beach your hotel or villa is, and whether there are any steps or busy roads to negotiate (in the Algarve many villas are on top of the cliffs with steep steps down). Never rely on just one source of information. In a holiday brochure, unless you can actually see the hotel and the beach in the same picture you can assume there'll be some sort of walk! Compare the same resort and beach in a couple of tour operators' brochures. Bear in mind too that a tiny sandy bay you have to yourselves with a shallow area of sea, perhaps protected by rocks, will be just as suitable for young children as a vast beach packed with other people.

The most reliable source of accurate information about overseas beaches is hidden in the resort reports published in the consumer magazine *Holiday Which?* (on subscription from Consumers' Association or most libraries will have a copy). You can also get detailed information from Meon Villas who produce their own comprehensive booklets on beaches in Menorca and on the Algarve, highlighting those that are suitable for under 8's.

There are some beaches in Europe that have been tried and tested by families for years. The following are a selection (there are many, many more), of clean, easy to get down to beaches

All you need is a buggy, a bucket, a sun umbrella . . .

that have decent sand and that shelve gently into the sea. Do bear in mind that beaches can change from year to year as far as cleanliness and shifting sand are concerned. Florida, of course, has excellent beaches as do many of the islands in the Caribbean.

Family Beaches Abroad

Black Sea

Bulgaria—Golden Sands and Sunny Beach
Romania—Mamaia

France

West Coast—Brittany, La Baule, and further south in the Vendée, Les Sables d'Olonne (seas can get rough).

Greece

Islands with suitable beaches include: Paros, Corfu, Rhodes. Also the Halkidiki peninsula on the mainland

Italy

Adriatic Riviera—Rimini, Cattolica, Pesaro, Riccione and Milano Marittima
Tuscany Coast—Viareggio
Venetian Riviera—Lido di Jesolo
South of Naples—Santa Maria di Castellabate (small)
Sicily—Cefalu

Portugal

Algarve—Albufeira, Faro and others (but seas can get rough and there may be steps to negotiate)

Spain

Costa Blanca—Benidorm, twin arcs of soft sand, 4 miles long
Costa Brava—Estartit, Tamariu
Costa Dorada—Salou
Ibiza—Playa D'En Bossa, Cala Llonga, Portinax
Majorca—Alcudia, Calla Millor, Cala Bona, Camp de Mar, Magaluf, Playa de Palma
Minorca—many safe and sandy beaches, sand dunes

Tunisia

Monastir

Yugoslavia

Best shallow shelving stretch at Ulcinj (8 miles long) and at Becici, both in the southern region of Montenegro

12
WINTER SUN
& LONGHAUL
DESTINATIONS

Winter Sun

Although many of the winter sun holiday brochures are covered in pictures of ladies in bikinis, much of Europe is too chilly for sunbathing outside June to September. Obviously you have to go a lot further afield than you would do in the summer to get real sunshine, although in southern Greece, Crete and Cyprus, North Africa, southern Spain and southern Portugal the sun can still be quite strong in October—maximum 66°F on the Algarve. The Algarve is often thought of as an off season destination but maximum temperatures only get up to the mid fifties from December to March, although they reach the early sixties by April. Majorca is warmer: December and January and February (almond blossom) can be in the mid sixties and by Easter the maximum daily temperature is 73°F. Do not expect to be able to swim in the sea early in the year, particularly the Atlantic which takes a lot longer to warm up than the Mediterranean. Mind you, the sea abroad in winter is probably no chillier than it is here during an English summer, and if the kids can go in then, in theory they could probably brave the elements anywhere in Europe!

To get really hot, swimming-in-the-sea weather, you will have to go to the Canaries (max 72°F at Christmas, max 70°F from January to March), Madeira (rocky beaches, so not very suitable), the Gambia, Israel (Eilat), Florida, the Caribbean or even further afield.

Longhaul Destinations

If you are planning to take the children outside Europe you may need inoculations (see health, p. 165). Some vaccinations (like yellow fever) are not recommended for children under 1 year old. To go to The Gambia, the Ivory Coast, Kenya and Israel for example, (all popular package tour destinations), you are recommended to have vaccinations against cholera, typhoid and polio and to take anti-malaria tablets in all of them except Israel. Since you can happily go to Florida, Spain, Greece, the Caribbean or the Canaries without having to have any jabs at all, this may well influence your choice of destination if you are taking young children.

Tour Operators

There may be genuinely free offers for children, during the autumn, spring and winter months, although you usually have to get in quick, and book as soon as you see the winter sun brochures appear (as early as June!).

The following are some suggestions of holidays suitable for families that operate during the winter. Also look up self-catering, activity holidays and holiday villages for other suggestions:

Club Méditerranée (see p. 116): Lots of winter sun destinations with miniclubs in hot and exotic places, including: Indonesia, New Caledonia, Israel, Bahamas, Brazil, Thailand, Dominican Republic, Florida, Mexico and Malaysia. Check your dates carefully as the miniclubs only operate during the French school holidays which can be different to ours.

Cosmos: Jimbo's OK Club for 2–12's operates in Tenerife. Good reductions for children up to 15.

No jabs needed for the Caribbean.

HCI: Southern Spain and Tenerife. Apartments and hotels. Good deals for single parents. Special Interest weeks: bowling, bridge, tennis, photography, darts, painting, golf and sequence dancing. Pirate's Club and nursery for babies.

La Manga, southern Spain: All year round leisure centre, 60 miles south of Alicante. Tennis, golf, all sorts of sports facilities and a miniclub during the school holidays for 2–17's.

Sol Hotels (see hotels, p. 89): All year round, but have good offers during the winter (sometimes free car hire and free places for children), single parents also qualify. 100 hotels throughout Spain and the Balearics.

Thomson: 3–11's can join the Big T Club with games and entertainment for three hours a day, four days a week. (Tunisia, Malta, Majorca, Canaries and southern Spain.)

Tradewinds: Free or cheap holiday offers to children to the Caribbean during certain months. See Country by Country, p. 57.

USA: California or Florida: Disney World, lots of options, lots of operators. See USA under Country by Country, p. 66.

13

SKIING

'Skiing holidays are best for babies because they have this little place that you can put them in all day.' (Laura, 7)

Many ski resorts in France, Austria, Switzerland, Spain and Italy are well geared up for families, especially the newer purpose-built ones. Many have excellent kindergartens where English-speaking staff will take care of your children for a day or half day at a time, leaving you free to hit the slopes. Some of the kinder-gartens are for babies and non-skiing children with an organised programme of activities. Most countries have nurseries for very young babies (Austria on the whole only takes over 3's or 'dry' ones). The babies are fed and changed and there are usually little cots for them to sleep in.

There are also kindergartens for children who want to learn to ski and they will be taken all together for lessons on the slopes. You pay a daily or weekly fee which often includes meals. These kindergartens are attached to the resort itself, so the children will meet others from neighbouring hotels, and nationalities will be mixed. A few tour operators have their own mini ski clubs (see below) in which all the children will be English.

If you are keen that your children learn to ski, tour operators will tell you the most suitable places. Some resorts have good reductions in children's ski schools and reductions on ski lifts. It varies considerably from resort to resort. You may find it more difficult to find suitable resorts for children in Italy, Andorra and the French and Spanish Pyrénées. The Swiss are probably the most generous with their reductions for children (up to 16 in some cases); the French probably the meanest.

Individual tour operators or the National Tourist Board of the country you are planning to visit will provide details of ski resorts with kindergartens and other facilities for children.

Tour operators who offer ski resorts suitable for families include:

Freedom Holidays specialise in family skiing in Andorra with baby clubs and kindergartens with English, trained nannies, children's ski school, babysitting and special meal times.

Small World have family chalet parties (cheapest if you can get a few families to go together) with a special ski-nanny to look after non-skiing under 4's on three days a week from 9—5 and until 2pm on two days. Over 4's will be escorted to the children's ski school, collected and given lunch in the chalet and entertained on three afternoons a week.

Thomson have a number of family resorts in their winter ski brochure with information about day and ski kindergartens, resorts offering children's (free or reduced cost) lift passes, and resorts where children's skis can be hired at a reduced cost.

Other Operators: Ski Sunmed (Auntie Snowflake clubs), Cosmos Skirama (ski kindergartens in Austria), Club Méditerranée (miniclubs in Switzerland, France and Italy), Crystal Holidays (Austria), PGL Family Skiing (Austria), Neilsons and Ski Nat (coach or air, miniclubs for 3—12's in Austria—snowman building, toboggan race, etc.). There are sometimes free holidays for children if they share your room, although there are usually only a limited number available so you have to book up early.

The best guide is *The Good Skiing Guide* (Consumers' Association and Hodder & Stoughton). It covers Europe's 200 best winter sports resorts and gives all the major resorts a rating as to their suitability for families. It also gives detailed information on discounts you can expect on ski lifts for children, whether the kindergartens are for skiing or non-skiing children, their costs, and the age of child they take.

Provisions for children on skiing holidays are much better than you might have expected.

14
CRUISES &
BOATS

The thought of being stuck on a ship with your children for weeks, with no means of escape apart from overboard or scheduled ports of call, might not sound like a good idea. Cruises have generally in the past been geared to older passengers happy to sit about in deckchairs. However, some cruise lines make a big effort for families and provide good reductions as well as all sorts of on board activities to stop children getting bored.

Cruise Companies

Canberra Cruises are particularly suitable for families with young children—parents complain they don't see enough of them! And they have the cheapest prices around. Ships operate Junior Clubs for 2–11's from 9am to 7pm. Trained hostesses organise fun and games, cartoons, discos, etc. Early mealtimes, cots, highchairs and special menus plus a night nursery. Youth Activities Officers take care of older children. Cruises from 8 to 20 days around the Mediterranean, Norway and the Canaries. From April to December. Under 3's get 90 per cent reductions if they are in a cot; 1–11's 75 per cent; 12–16's 50 per cent off; 17–20 year olds 40 per cent off. Special family cabins, or two children would get their own. On Princess Cruises, more luxurious ships that cruise to more exotic locations, 2–12's get 50 per cent off but basic prices higher and there are no special facilities for children.

Royal Caribbean have four ships with 7, 8, 10 or 14 day cruises from Miami around the Caribbean (great beaches when you get there). On departures during the summer holidays, Christmas and New Year they have Kid/Teen programmes on board with activities for children from 6−12 and from 13−17. Youth leaders organise games and sports (everything from kite flying to putting), plus ice-cream and pizza parties, kids films and discos. At ports they will take children off to places of interest. Reductions for children plus special offers (like free flights to Miami) and the possibility of add-on trips to Disney World and the Kennedy Space Centre.

Boating Holidays

UK

Somewhat less ambitious than a cruise is a boating holiday. You can rent anything from a fully equipped cruiser to a narrowboat with anything from two to twelve berths. Nearly all boats come as well equipped as a holiday cottage, often with their own loos and fridges, ovens, cooking utensils, TV's and central heating. You can cruise the Broads, the Thames and umpteen canals and rivers, navigating yourself or taking it easy on a hotel boat. Don't be put off if you have no experience, they will tell you how to do it at the boatyard.

Some children might get a bit bored with the pace of life on a boat and small children may feel very restrained and restricted. But negotiating locks, stopping for picnics and barbecues, or to peddle off along the towpath does appeal to lots of children. It is probably not a good idea to do this sort of holiday with a toddler or with children who cannot swim. Boating holidays in Britain bookable through British Waterways, who manage 2,000 miles of Britain's canals and rivers, Hoseasons and Blakes. The English Tourist Board's *Hobby and Activity Holidays* lists other operators.

Abroad

Blakes also have narrow boats, and houseboats, on the canals of France, in Ireland, Holland and Denmark. You travel in your own car or by air. Children up to 13 or 15 travel free at specific times depending on ferry company and destination. And under 4's or 5's travel free at all times.

Brittany Ferries have their own canal cruisers on the canals of France.

Hoseasons boats have boating holidays on the canals of France, and Holland, and in Denmark. Disabled passengers are accommodated on one of their Dutch canal boats.

15

ACCOMMODATION

UK

'Mummy and Daddy like hotels because of the beds.'
(Katy, 5)

According to *The Peaudouce Guide* (to 2,000 hotels, pubs and restaurants that welcome children), one in four hotels in this country ban children altogether!

Fortunately, hotels that do welcome children mean it, and most provide the necessities for a good family holiday: cots, highchairs, playrooms, early suppers, and children's menus, games rooms, gardens and babysitting. Finding these hotels isn't always easy; what you need is a good guidebook (see below).

Outside the summer holidays there are often special packages available, which might make taking a long weekend or half-term break tempting. The English Tourist Board's *Let's Go* details hotels offering short breaks in England during autumn, winter and spring, at reduced rates. You may get discounted railfares, tickets for museums, and some sort of theme thrown in. Theme weekends are becoming increasingly popular; subjects range from all sorts of sports, with tuition, to wine appreciation, gardens, health and fitness, painting or murder!

Good travel agents should have brochures of the larger hotel chains or contact individual hotels in the *Let's Go* guide direct.

Hotel Chains

The other way of ensuring you get good facilities is to choose a hotel chain that has a policy of welcoming families. Free holidays for children are quite common, but with most of them (though not all) they have to share your bedroom. Be prepared to be cramped and you may be pleasantly surprised. Meals are usually extra, though a few include breakfast, and many have special children's menus. Mostly these offers are with the larger hotel chains, sometimes restricted to weekends or off season breaks. As well as the free accommodation you may also get free rail travel thrown in.

One, not so small point. Hotel chains often have special children's menus in their restaurants. Although plenty of kids *like* beans, chips, fish fingers and sausages, plenty of parents spend lots of time trying to get their children eating food that has rather more nutritional value and try and keep down the amount of sweets they eat. I don't know about you but enticing offers of free sweets and lollipops to children by some restaurants actually put *me* off! How about free crunchy bars or raisins hoteliers!

Among hotel chains with the best offers for families are.

Best Western: Large chain of independently owned hotels, so all different. Lots at seasides. Getaway Breaks are the best value and two children under 15 can share their parents' room free (provided they eat breakfast and dinner in the hotel). Wide range of sports and activity breaks.

Consort Hotels: Up to two children under 16 stay free if sharing with parents at some hotels. Activity holidays. 220 independent hotels.

Crest Hotels: Up to three children under 14 can stay free in a *separate* family room when accompanied by two adults. Special Welcome Breaks at specific hotels with supervised activities for Whizz Kids: games room with toys (weekends), supper trays, videos, babysitting. Multi-activity weekends, adventure weekends and children's computer weekends at selected hotels on specific dates. London, cities and seasides. Similar offers at hotels in Europe.

Embassy Hotels: Over 60 hotels all over Britain. Special Interest breaks. Up to two children under 16 can share your room (if it's big enough) free. Children's menus or 50 per cent off meals.

Golden Rail: Packages by rail and coach. Self-catering and hotels, special summer by the sea brochure. Under 5's free at hotels when sharing, 50 per cent reductions for under 15's when sharing your room.

Highlife Breaks (Thistle Hotels): Under 14's free. Family hotels. Also activities.

Holiday Inns: On Weekender packages children under 19 stay

Scarlett with her constant companion.

Give them a Coke and an ice-cream and they'll follow you anywhere.

free, providing they share with two parents; meals for 12's and under half price. Children under 16 can get free rail travel. Family Weekenders additionally provide membership to the Johnny Holiday Club. Fun and games in the Club room, pool, baby patrolling, magic and film shows, fun bag and free entrance tickets to local attractions. Mostly city hotels.

Inter Hotels: Independent hotels. Children under 14 can share with parents free at a large number, including Wales. Activity breaks and car tours.

Ladbroke Hotels: Children under 14 free when sharing with parents. Weekend breaks.

Quality International: Budget Breaks. Eight hotels, including Blackpool and Scarborough. Free accommodation if sharing for under 15's, and free meals also for under 5's. Children automatically become members of the Percy Pudding Club with special menus, gifts and follow-up birthday cards. Older children might enjoy their ghoulish Murder & Mystery or Dracula weekends. Half price rail travel for under 14's, free for under 5's.

Queens Moat Houses: Town and Country Classic weekends. Up to two children under 14 stay free if sharing with adults.

Rainbow Mini Holidays: Over 70 hotels including seasides and London. Up to two children under 16 free accommodation (sharing with parents) and rail travel.

Stardust and Camelot Mini Holidays: In Great Britain and Jersey. Under 15's stay free and get free breakfast at some hotels. Leisure facilities at lots of hotels.

Superbreak Mini Holidays: Over 200 hotels (including London and Ireland). Up to two children under 16 can share your room free and get free rail travel. At discretion of hotel a child travelling with one adult can also stay free. Special breaks and activities.

Trusthouse Forte: Nearly 200 hotels all over Britain, lots by the sea, especially in the West Country. Children under 16 can share a room with you, free. Hungry Bear children's menus and Bumper Funcases (games, colouring books, pens). Small number of family favourite hotels, several in the West Country with additional features like paddling pools and crèches. Babyfoods, cots and highchairs available. All-inclusive breaks with free travel by rail or coach.

Pubs and Inns

There is nothing worse on holiday than lunchtime in the country and arriving at a pub to find they won't let your children through the door. I've even been turned away on my own with a toddler in a winter snowstorm from a country pub in Somerset! Such are the British licensing laws.

Although pubs prohibit children under 14 from drinking in the bar area, many pubs do welcome children and provide family rooms for them to eat in as well as stay in, and swings and amusements outside. Many pubs are beautifully situated near the sea or in the heart of the countryside.

Guidebooks

England's Seaside (English Tourist Board). Lists hundreds of seaside hotels and guesthouses whose owners have signed a declaration that they welcome children, they are all within easy distance of the sea and have to provide a set list of necessities like cots, highchairs, toys, early suppers, somewhere to warm bottles and babysitting.

The Family Welcome Guide (Sphere). A fat book with a large number of entries with detailed descriptions of all the suitable facilities for families. It also includes restaurants, and pubs, that have family rooms, gardens and games rooms.

The Peaudouce Guide (Peaudouce). A slim volume of 2,000 reasonably priced inns, hotels, pubs and restaurants, with fairly brief descriptions. Only available by mail order (29 Priory Street, Ware, Herts.).

Other guides worth having with you if you are looking for a pub that welcomes children include those produced by Courage Inns, whose brochure lists their pubs where you can stay in in Devon and Cornwall, including those that welcome children under 14 and have family rooms. The slim Benson and Hedges *Stay at an Inn* guide, (distributed by the AA and published by the British Tourist Authority) gives a rocking horse symbol against pubs and inns that welcome children.

You could also refer to the enormously helpful and fat *Good Pub Guide* (Consumers' Association). It's available in bookshops. It's editor, Alisdair Aird, has personally inspected thousands of pubs all over the country and points out those that have family rooms and welcome children. Egon Ronay's *Guinness Pub Guide* (published by the AA) also includes pubs that cater for children.

Abroad

On the whole hotels abroad are a lot more enthusiastic about having children to stay than they are in this country and the larger chains have good concessions, with plenty of offers of free accommodation if the children share your room. Some countries also have national pricing policies for families. For example, in Portugal, children under 8 are entitled to a discount of 50 per cent in all hotels if they share a room with the person accompanying them.

A large number of tour operators also have good facilities for children in the hotels they use abroad, installing their own miniclubs and supervisors (see p. 69).

Lancaster Family First Holidays offer a unique arrangement at several of the hotels they use abroad: in conjunction with Mothercare, they have equipped hotels they use in Spain (mainland and Majorca), also one in Italy and one in Portugal, with Mothercare Units stocking Mothercare products and run by English nurses and nannies. The Units have washing machines, a cooker, sinks, irons, potties, and bottle warming and sterilising facilities. There is also a shop selling a range of Mothercare equipment: nappies, creams and lotions, feeding bottles, etc. (no food or milk). The hotels have Mothercare cots and high-chairs, and you can hire out buggies with sun umbrellas. There are also laundries, mini-bar, playrooms. Hotels with these facilities have been checked for safety of lifts, pools, sockets, fire escapes and balconies.

Specially trained nurses and nannies look after babies (no less than four hours a day). For older children a First Mates Club (3–12's) runs for three hours a day, six days a week with supervised activities and outings.

Hotel Chains

If you are planning to tour abroad, ask the National Tourist Office in this country whether they know about any chains of hotels with special schemes for visitors. You can often get pre-bookable vouchers or hotel cheques in advance, entitling you to discounts. A number of hotel chains have good facilities.

Crest, who have around 90 hotels in Britain, Germany, Holland, Belgium, Italy and Austria are particularly good for families in that their free offers of accommodation apply even if your children sleep in a separate room; up to three can stay free if they travel with two adults at selected hotels. They also give children a fun and games pack, special menus and Crest cocktails like Pink Piggy (orange juice and grenadine with soda). Lots of their hotels also have leisure clubs.

The following are a selection of hotel chains within different countries with particularly good deals for families.

France

Novotels: A chain of 3★ hotels, half of which are in France (also worldwide), allow children under 16 to share your room free, and they get free breakfasts.

Sofitels: 4★ hotels also mostly in France, allow one child under

12 to share your room for nothing but in recent years during July and August have allowed up to three children to have their own room for nothing—and there's no age limit, so theoretically parents with their parents would qualify!

Germany

Dorint Hotels: Some have fully equipped nurseries. All have playrooms and offer films, paints, crayons with special menus in the restaurants, highchairs and Mickey Mouse.

Israel

The IRH chain of hotels offer 3–13's at specific times special children's programmes and have free offers of accommodation. See Peltours brochure.

Scandinavia

There are several discounted hotel schemes available in Scandinavia but you have to buy them in advance (details from individual Tourist Boards). The Scandinavian Bonus Pass allows good discounts (15 to 40 per cent) at over 114 first class hotels. Children under 15 can share with their parents free and get free breakfast too. Children under 15 also stay free (under 6's get free breakfast) at Scandic Hotels during specific periods. Bookings through Best Western.

Spain

Sol Hotels: The largest hotel group in Spain with over 90 hotels in major resorts and cities. They are featured in most of the package tour brochures to Spain or you can book independently through Utell International. Kids' Centres operate in specific hotels in Majorca and Torremolinos for babies and toddlers up to 4. Each centre is supervised by a nurse, you can warm up milk and meals, there's a fridge, babybaths, potties, playpens, pushchairs and a baby shop. Highchairs are available in the restaurants and baby patrolling in the evening. For 5–11's all Sol Hotels in holiday areas run miniclubs with organised activities, competitions, shows, excursions, cabarets and videos. Teenagers have their own clubs with sporting events and discos. Parents are offered a wide range of sports to choose from and holiday courses in cooking, flower arranging, or making cocktails. Evening entertainment includes live shows, talent contests, games and themes. You can opt in or out.

Switzerland

The Swiss National Tourist Office have a booklet of suitable hotels for families, all members of the Swiss Hotel Association. Hotels have symbols denoting children's menus, supervised playrooms (4 hours a day), play areas, etc. Up to 6's free, 6–12's half price if sharing a parent's room. Also Happy Family Swiss Hotels run special circus familiarisation courses for children at a number of hotels. (Contact Happy Family Swiss Hotels, 8784 Braunwald, Switzerland.) Dorint Hotels have films and play-rooms for children, crayons in the restaurants, special menus and highchairs. The Movenpick chain allow children under 16 to share free with one or more parent.

USA

In the States you are charged for the room rather than per person. Since most hotel and motel rooms have two large king-sized beds this can work out very cheaply if you don't all mind bunking in together. Several hotel chains in the States also offer packages (weekends or weekly terms) for families where children under 18 can share your room for nothing. There are too many hotel chains to list them all here, but Days Inns as well as letting children share your room for nothing also offer under 12's free food from special menus (motels all over the States including Florida). Visit USA vouchers are available in advance.

Hawai: Aston Hotels have 22 hotels at resort complexes on five islands. 8–12's get a free activity programme at six West Maui properties. Activities for parents and children include sailing, volcanic crater hikes, riding, scuba diving and helicopter tours. Children under 18 sharing with parents stay free. (Contact Destination Marketing. Tel: 01 637 7961.)

To book a hotel abroad you can either write or ring direct or go through an agency. One of the largest is: Utell, Banda House, Cambridge Grove, London W6. Tel: 01 741 1588.

16
SHORT
BREAKS

Although by law you are not allowed to take school age kids out of school for more than two weeks of term time, you may want to take them away during the Easter and Christmas holidays, for half-terms and long weekends, either in this country or abroad.

UK

In Britain a large number of hotels reduce their rates dramatically from September to around May and offer all sorts of weekend breaks at attractive prices for families, with a wide range of activities thrown in. The best source of what's available is the English Tourist Board's *Let's Go* publication which covers short breaks at reduced rates in England. Their *Activity & Hobby Holidays* lists hundreds of special interest and sporting holidays suitable for families, many of which run during the Easter holidays.

Hotel chains and operators with year round programmes of activities or special facilities for children include: Trusthouse Forte, Crest, Consort, Embassy, Golden Rail, Highlife Breaks (Thistle), Holiday Inn, Best Western, Rainbow Mini Holidays, Stardust and Camelot Mini Holidays, Superbreak Mini Holidays, Queens Moat Houses (Town & Country Classics) and Quality International.

Abroad

If you are taking a holiday abroad during a half-term, Easter or Christmas, the chances are you are either planning to visit a city, or to take the car to Northern Europe. (For Skiing and Winter Sun see pages 79 and 76 respectively.)

Across the Channel

Most of the ferry companies package up short trips where you take your own car. There are always good reductions for children (see p. 153), sometimes quite old children can stay free if they share your room and there are quite a lot of places worth going to for just a few days. See the entries under each country (p. 49) to give you inspiration.

Cities

There are no short breaks abroad specifically geared up for children but a large number of tour operators have packages to cities in Europe. Most children under 10 wouldn't get a lot out of them, although, of course, you might. You have to compromise if you are taking kids to cities and be prepared to take things at a slow pace. So long as you don't expect them to follow you anywhere and be happy about it, you should get at least as much enjoyment out of a trip abroad as you would spending a weekend doing the sights of London! Obviously there are plenty of attractions in most cities abroad for children, so long as you don't mind using up valuable sightseeing time in visiting them. Children from 5 upwards would enjoy Paris, for example, as long as you were prepared to go up the Eiffel Tower, on a Bâteau Mouche and spend some hours at the Beaubourg (clowns, magicians, magic and music). Kids of all ages would love the Tivoli Gardens in Copenhagen, or Amsterdam in springtime to see the bulbfields. Check with National Tourist Offices about special museum tickets. Sometimes you get substantial reductions on family tickets or if you buy tickets in advance.

17
SELF-CATERING

'It's not as expensive and you don't have people coming into you all the time, and you can go out when you like, if it wasn't self-catering you would have to stay in and have your meals there.' (Paul, 5)

Self-catering means freedom. Having your own kitchen sink, whether you use it much or not, is considered essential by millions of families fed up with the restrictions of life in hotels. You can get up when you like, feed the baby at 2 in the morning, scramble up some eggs when your toddler wants his supper, bunk your teenagers down in the sitting room (often for nothing) and make as much noise as you want to without the management disapproving and the people in the room next door banging on the wall to tell you to keep the sound down.

People who have never self-catered before often haven't because they think they are going to be tied to the kitchen sink. People who have, know that they spend a lot of time in the local farm shop or deli, buying cheese, salami, fruit and bread, and frequently eat out. Most self-caterers use their kitchen sink for the kids and breakfast, and the fridge for keeping drinks cold.

If you want your privacy you can choose to be miles from anywhere, in the middle of a forest, on a clifftop. If you like having other people around, you can opt for a holiday village or complex of flats or apartments with on site swimming pools, playgrounds, restaurants, bars, entertainment, launderettes and, most importantly, other children for yours to play with. There's nothing guaranteed to give you more freedom than your kids making friends.

The choice of property is enormous. In Britain you can rent a caravan in a holiday camp, a tiny windswept croft in the Outer Hebrides, a flat in a wing of a stately home, a thatched cottage in a country lane, or a modern bungalow by the sea. Abroad there are exclusive villas in the Caribbean that come with their own butler, maid and gardener, studios in tiny fishing villages in the Mediterranean, wings of châteaux or *gîtes* in rural spots of France, large family villas with their own pools in Spain, apartments in castles, palaces and old farmhouses in Italy, log cabins in Sweden, and luxury caravans on sites all over Europe.

If you want to compromise you can rent yourself a flat in an aparthotel, a cross between a flat and a hotel. You can rustle up meals at a convenient time for the children and then have dinner in the hotel's restaurant when they are in bed. There are a large number of them in Spain, in Portugal's Algarve and in nothern Europe, and they really do give you the best of both worlds with pools, indoor and outdoor play areas, babysitters if you need them, and, should you want them, early mealtimes and highchairs in the restaurant.

Most properties in this country and abroad are sold in brochures according to the number of people they will sleep. Do not assume that 'sleeps 4' means in two bedrooms. Often you will find that the sofa in the living room converts into a bed. You may also find that the table folds up to make room for it. Most properties will supply a cot and a highchair if you ask them in advance, although you may have to pay a small amount locally for them. Holiday costs are based on the cost of renting the whole property and it often doesn't matter how many people you take, although in some cases there is a maximum. The more of you that travel together, the cheaper it is.

UK

British hoteliers are not renowned for their sympathetic attitude to the normal behaviour of youngsters, which is why self-catering is so popular.

You can either choose your property through an agency, a lot of whom package up holiday homes into a brochure rather like a tour operator's, or you can rent privately through small ads. in your local or the Sunday papers. The disadvantage of doing it all yourself is that you have to take what they say about the place on trust. With an agency the property will have been inspected and they do the booking for you.

As you pay for the property itself, not per person, provided there are enough beds you can holiday pretty cheaply, especially if some of the kids are happy sleeping in a sleeping bag. Sometimes you take your own linen, sometimes it's supplied. You may or may not be able to take the dog. Most will also provide cots, highchairs, plus games, packs of cards and books for rainy days. Some even have videos and stereos, microwave ovens and dishwashers. Since almost all self-catering properties are privately owned, no two are alike.

Self-catering in Britain is also covered in other chapters of this book: on farms (see p. 102) at holiday centres (see p. 112) and on caravan sites (see p. 107). Most self-catering complexes have playgrounds, playleaders, babysitting, pools, competitions, sports and activities. Lots of other children around, plus bars and restaurants so you don't have to cook a thing.

Self-catering Holiday Companies—UK

The following are a selection out of an enormous list of self-catering companies. Those I have picked cover different areas of Britain, and often have unusual properties in unusual places. Most will provide cots and highchairs for children, on request.

Blakes: Specialise in boating holidays but also have a wide range of properties inland and by the sea. England, Scotland, Wales and Ireland. Cheap rail travel.

Cabin Holidays: Sister company of Canvas Holidays (camping abroad). Luxury pine self-catering cabins in England, Scotland and Wales with their own development on the Isle of Skye.

Cerbid Quality Cottages: 60 properties along the Welsh coastline and inland (from 600 inspected). Also properties in Devon and Cornwall. Many suitable for families.

English Country Cottages: Separate brochures for England, Scotland and Wales. Over 1,500 up market, quality properties on their books, from cottages and farmhouses to complete country mansions. Some have extensive grounds. Also 'cottage collections'—groups of cottages under one owner with their own exclusive pools and leisure centres.

Foresty Commission: Forest cabins and holiday houses in forested areas from Scotland to Cornwall. Cabins, stone cottages, timber built houses, some with open fires. Cots can be provided.

Helpful Holiday Agency: Personal service is their speciality. All the properties are in the West Country, by the sea, on farms, on the Moors. They star rate properties, can get cots and highchairs and will help if you are indecisive.

Hoseasons: Specialise in boating and holiday homes in England, Scotland and Wales. Wide range of properties from a medieval castle in Wales to a Spanish style holiday village next to the Camelot theme park (see p. 51) in Lancashire. Good savings on travel.

Landmark Trust: The Trust is dedicated to finding and refurbishing properties of character and history. Wide range of unusual properties from an eighteenth century tower in Yorkshire to a medieval manor house near Leeds.

National Trust: Have a collection of holiday cottages that range enormously in size and comfort, from a spartan fell cottage in the Lake District to a manor house in West Wales. All are in superb locations and in unspoilt settings. Information and bookings are divided into areas.

Abroad

Self-catering holidays abroad offer some of the best deals for families. On self-catering holidays the free offers for children are often available throughout the year, rather than restricted to term time. Also tour operators are more generous with their upper limit of children's ages, with good discounts for children up to 16 rather than the usual 11 or 12. The Travel Club of Upminster, who specialise in villas and apartments in Portugal's Algarve, will let children up to 20 travel for 50 per cent of the holiday price, provided they are prepared to bunk down in the living room.

Food and its Cost Abroad

'You don't *have* to do cooking or anything, that's what Mummy says.' (Katy, 5)

Some people who self-cater abroad eat out all the time, only using their kitchen for the children or for breakfast. If you want to do more than scramble up a few eggs it is well worth investing in a self-catering guide to the local food and drink. There are five titles in the Christopher Helm series: *Self-Catering in France*, *Italy*, *Spain*, *Portugal* and *Greece*. As well as explaining the local produce, menus, markets and wines the guides also devote a section to travelling with children.

When you are choosing a country to self-cater in, it is worth thinking about how much food is going to cost when you get there. Last summer Thomas Cook published a shopping basket of food costs based on the cost of buying food in some of the resorts they go to: Portugal, Corfu, Costa del Sol, Cyprus, Majorca, Rhodes, Tenerife and Yugoslavia.

They found that:

Butter was three times as expensive in Yugoslavia as it is here, and more than double in Majorca and the Costa del Sol. Butter cost more than it does here in Portugal and Corfu, but was cheaper in Rhodes, Tenerife and Cyprus.

Cheese was very expensive in the Costa del Sol, Majorca and Tenerife.

Eggs were quite a bit more expensive in Corfu, the cheapest place was Cyprus; everywhere else was about the same as here.
Milk was cheaper everywhere abroad in the survey than in the UK.
Meat: pork was almost double in Majorca and Portugal and a lot cheaper in Cyprus. Lamb was cheaper everywhere (very cheap in Rhodes and Yugoslavia), except Tenerife where it was very expensive.
Tomatoes were cheaper everywhere than here.
Tea was more than double in the Costa del Sol and Majorca, and still a lot more in Portugal and Tenerife. The only place where it was cheaper than here was in Rhodes.
Beer was cheaper everywhere abroad except Rhodes where it was a bit more expensive. Very cheap in Portugal and Majorca.
Wine was cheaper everywhere abroad. Cheapest places were the Costa del Sol, Majorca and Yugoslavia.

Overall Thomas Cook found that Cyprus was good value for food, and Rhodes and Corfu were cheap too, certainly cheaper than here. You can, of course, self-cater as far afield as the Caribbean but most food, except locally grown fruit, is expensive there. Most of it is imported from the States. Local shops may not appeal to you, although there will be masses of fresh fruit and vegetables in the markets.

Type of Property

The standards of holiday homes and the type of property varies considerably from country to country. In France, for example, rustic simplicity is the key word (unless you are renting a flat in a château); in Spain you can expect high standards of furnishings and decor in expensive resorts or pokey rabbit warrens, thousands of them all the same, in the cheaper ones; in Portugal villas and apartments will be clean and bright with lots of ceramic tiles; in Italy you'll find rustic farmhouses inland and sophisticated villas in parts of Sardinia; in Greece you'll be spending a lot of time out of doors, which is a jolly good thing because your holiday home may only run to a couple of bent forks in the drawers and a plastic chair to have your dinner on.

Brochure language can be a bit misleading. 'Villa' doesn't always mean a detached property but could be part of a house divided up into different units. 'Studio' usually means one room with cooking facilities in the corner and a sofa that converts into a bed. 'Sleeps 6' often means two bedrooms and a put-u-up in the living room. You can request cots and highchairs; there may be a small charge to pay locally.

A word of warning. At the more expensive end of the market you can hire villas that come with their own swimming pools. If you are holidaying with younger children who either can't swim or have just learnt, it is better to rent a villa where the pool is fenced off. You will not get a moment's rest if you have to watch out continually in case your child wanders too near the edge.

Take Your Own Car

You often need a car on a self-catering holiday. Most of the ferry companies package up all-inclusive holidays that include the price of the crossing and the property. The more of you that travel together the cheaper it is. A lot of holiday homes are within easy reach of the boat terminals: not just France and Spain but Scandinavia and Ireland too: summerhouses, log cabins, *gîtes*, bungalows, apartments, villas, caravans, and tents. There are some very good deals for families. Most of the ferry operators allow children under 4 to travel free, and some offer them free accommodation too. Even if it isn't completely free you may only have to pay a nominal amount. It may be tempting, just because the kids go free, to cram the car full of them. However, if you choose a property that involves a long drive you'll probably need a good week to recover from the journey. With a carload of passengers it's best to select a holiday home that isn't far from the ferry terminal.

Packages: Hoverspeed Continental Motoring Holidays, Brittany Ferries and DFDS Longship (Scandinavia and Germany) (see below), Sealink (under 14's free to nothern Europe, under 16's free to Ireland), B&I line (under 16's free on holidays in Ireland).

Tour Operators

Almost all the larger tour operators have a selection of self-catering properties. Sometimes they are in a separate brochure sometimes mixed up with hotels in the main brochure. The big companies (like Thomson and Sunmed) also run their special supervised miniclubs on self-catering holidays.

I can't list all of them here but I can pick out a few of the better deals, some of the more obscure properties and a few operators you might not know about. As usual, travel agents will have brochures, or look up the names of the company in the references on pp. 192–5.

Brittany Ferries package up hundreds of *gîtes* in France (see farms p. 102). They charge children (4–13) a nominal amount per week, and under 4's go free.

Center Parcs aren't terribly well-known here but their five star bungalow sites (in Holland and Belgium) cater exceptionally well for families. The play leaders speak English, they have supervised playrooms (3–12's), masses of activities going on, sophisticated subtropical swimming pools, and babysitting. The first British Center Parc is due to open in Sherwood Forest, Nottingham this year: a £32 million development, built with the help of an ETB grant. Bookings through Thomas Cook and Sealink.

Châteaux en France: Strictly if you are feeling extravagant and you've got kids who won't ruin the furniture! You can rent out wings of châteaux in most regions of France, sometimes a whole *manoir*. A maid will come in and clean for you. The price you pay is for the whole property so you can take as many people as you like. Several are suitable for families; cots and babysitting are available. Decor and furnishings are often of the highest standards; plus antiques and paintings. Grounds may include pools and tennis courts. You make your own way there, which is not so expensive if you choose a ferry company with good prices for children.

DFDS Longship Holidays specialise in holidays by DFDS ships to Denmark, Sweden, Germany and Norway. Self-catering properties include: in Denmark, traditional summerhouses (over 1,500 of them), bungalows and apartments in holiday centres with their own pools (often indoor), saunas, playgrounds and sports facilities. Some even have their own dishwashers. In Sweden: log cabins along river banks or by Sweden's numerous lakes (canoes and windsurfers to hire). In Norway: apartment hotels and cabins overlooking Norway's fjords. In Germany: holiday parks with bungalows in forests, by lakes and by the sea with excellent on site facilities, pools, playgrounds, tennis, etc. and riding or watersports nearby. The large apartment complex they offer in the Harz Mountains has a supervised kindergarten, minigolf, adventure playground and paddling pools.

Interhome is the company with the biggest choice with over 15,000 apartments, chalets and villas on their books, all over Europe. Their brochure gives a small picture of the property (anything from a chalet in Switzerland to a wing of a château in France, and every conceivable type of building in between). They book up for you and you can either take advantage of all-inclusive travel arrangements or make your own way there. They have a wide range of chalets and apartments in ski resorts as well as along Mediterranean beaches and inland. From time to time, particularly early or late in the season (good for half-terms), they come up with exceptionally cheap deals. It is worth asking about what they have on offer before you start wading through the brochures.

Meon Villas offer a range of villa holidays by air, price reductions aren't wonderful but a car is included on most holidays (not Greece) along with your own swimming pool. A good idea if you want to share with friends, if you have an enormous family or if you want to take the grandparents (babysitting?).

Scanhomes have self-catering summerhouses (and farms) in Denmark. Most Danes have a cottage that they retreat to at weekends—over 400 of them are on Scanhomes' books. Most are fairly simple, chalet style, built out of wood, with gardens. Some have thatched roofs. Lots on the beach (Denmark has vast expanses of good beaches, if somewhat windswept, particularly on the West coast of Jutland). Bunks for the kids. Free entry to Legoland and Tivoli. Since Danish children go back to school earlier than ours, you can holiday in August at low season prices. By sea with your own car or by air.

Wings-OSL have a wide range of villas and apartments throughout the Mediterranean, by air. They highlight the properties that are particularly suitable for children in their brochure, will supply cots free (comply with British Safety Standards) and will additionally supply details of whether disposable nappies, babyfood and powdered milk are available in the resorts they go to.

Before You Book

Whether you are planning a self-catering holiday in this country or abroad find out:

* How far the property is from: the nearest shop, restaurant, pub, bar, town or village. It is no fun to run out of milk or beer or to have to walk miles to get fresh bread for breakfast.
* How far the property is from the beach and what the access is like (busy road, unmade up path, steps).
* How many bedrooms there are, *not* just beds (you may find that the sofa converts into a bed and another one folds out of a wardrobe).
* Check layout of the property, where the bathroom is in relation to your child's bedroom, how steep the stairs are (can sometimes get stairgates in the UK).
* If there is an open fire, is there a fire guard?
* Check about cots, highchairs, toys, games; is there a TV?
* What the views are like.
* If there are any hazards for children (unfenced garden full of rosebushes, no gate around the pool, road outside, nearby river or pond, thistles, etc.).
* Compare the perks between properties: can collect own farm eggs, ride ponies, feed ducks, swings in garden, possible babysitters.

What to Take With You

If you are self-catering with a young family there are a few specific things you shouldn't forget to take with you (for fuller list, see packing on p. 182) including:

* Baby's dish, feeding spoon and beaker (bottles, etc.).
* A thermos for taking drinks to the beach and making up packets.
* A mouli or food grinder for mincing food.
* Sheets, blankets and plastic sheet for the cot.

* Straps (for highchair).
* Plastic mats.
* Travel highchair (if there isn't going to be one, or even for eating out in restaurants).
* Jars and packets of babyfood for travelling and emergencies (you can get more when you are there).
* Travel cot if they won't supply one.
* Lots of cloths and plastic bags (with ties).

18

FARMHOUSE HOLIDAYS

UK

'I got my own egg from the chicken for breakfast. It was warm. I don't like eggs, but those ones were lovely.'
(Jessica, 4)

For most city children, staying on a farm is a unique and educational experience. And it is one of the cheapest holidays you can have as a family. There are literally hundreds of farms in Britain that take in paying guests: sheep farms on the moors, dairy farms in the West Country, fruit farms in Kent. Many belong to small groups who have banded together to market themselves and to try and ensure that their farmhouses and what they offer their guests are up to scratch. But until the Farm Holidays Bureau was set up a few years ago there was no national co-ordinating body and to book you had to contact each regional group separately or try and find individual holiday operators. The Bureau, set up in conjunction with the English Tourist Board, now co-ordinates some 700 farms which they list with descriptions in their guide.

Staying on a British farm either means renting out a self-catering flat, often converted out of the stable block or derelict outbuildings, or staying as a guest in the main farmhouse. Usually there will be two or three spare bedrooms and a communal bathroom. Some farms have spent a lot of money improving their facilities and have added private bathrooms but don't get carried away, you can't expect the sort of service you get in a hotel! Farm holidays are far more personal. Usually the farmer's wife will go out of her way to make you feel at home.

102

Hello, what's going on in there?

Most children love staying on a farm.

Other guests may well be from abroad and, unlike hotels, everybody talks to each other! Breakfast will be early, usually before 9, you can sometimes help yourself to eggs, the bacon may be home-produced, the milk from the farm's own cows.

'The best bit was I stepped in cow's muck because I got my whole shoe in it.' (Lucy, 6)

Evening meals will often be available though at many farms it may be a bit too early for your liking, perhaps at 6 or 6.30. But in case you get peckish before bed there'll be tea and biscuits, or home-made scones to eat in the front room at around 9 or 10. There's almost always a telly, sometimes an open fire and loads of books, packs of cards and boardgames.

Children are more than welcome. On most farms they will get a reduced rate and few farmers object to normal boisterous behaviour. In fact most of the farms I've stayed in have stacks of games and books for children as well as farmhouse pets, perhaps a pony to ride, and swings in the garden. If you are keen to have animals around, check carefully in the various guides to see what's available, some farms are strictly mechanised. Or phone direct. Little children are far more interested in a couple of chickens, a rabbit, a goat and sundry cats and dogs than a field full of Friesians. If you want your children to see new born lambs or calves choose to stay in a farm during the Easter holidays. Phone a few first and ask them when their lambs are due. With any luck the children may even be allowed to help bottle feed them.

In the evening if you want to go out (say, down to the local pub after dinner, or just for a walk) the farmer's family will usually be around to babysit. Since the farm will most often be just a small house your children will probably feel quite secure. Many provide cots and highchairs and if you are lucky their kids will be the same age as yours—and you won't see them for dust. They may accommodate your own pets.

All sorts of other activities might be offered; including riding, sailing, fishing, and bikes to ride. Some farms provide their own farm trails, fruit picking and information sheets for children. Plus a whole stack of maps and brochures on what to do and see in the area, the loan of wellies, and packed lunches. Take a thermos, children's rucksacks and anoraks.

Brochures and Guidebooks

Individual regional tourist boards provide free brochures on farm holidays and will put you in touch with local groups in their region.

Farm Holidays in Britain (Farm Holiday Bureau in association with the English Tourist Board).
Farm Holiday Guide England and the Channel Islands (FHB).

Country Farm Holidays (a brochure with a selection of farm-house holidays and cottages on farms), free from Shaw Mews, Shaw Street, Worcester. Tel: 0905 613744.
Guesthouses, Farmhouses and Inns in Britain (AA).
The Wales Tourist Board includes farms in its *Wales Bed and Breakfast*, available from the tourist board and there are a number of local groups.
In Scotland, *Scottish Farmhouse Holidays and Crofts* are run as a consortium and carefully monitored, a selection are included in a brochure available from: Drumtenant, Ladybank, Fife. Tel: 0337 30451.
In Ireland, *Farm Holidays in Ireland* (Irish Farm Holidays Association). Book available from Ashton Grove, Knockraha, Co. Cork.

Abroad

You may be surprised to learn that farms abroad have been opening their doors to paying guests for a lot longer than we have. The set up is much the same, although you have the advantage of being in a foreign place when it comes to exploring the surrounding countryside; and home-cooking abroad can be a lot more interesting than the food you get at home. Individual National Tourist Boards have lists of farms in their country and what they offer. Countries in which farm tourism is well-established are:

Austria: Farms available near Salzburg in several small villages in the Salzkammergut Lake District. DER have packages with your own car. Also the Austrian Tourist Board produce detailed brochures on farmhouse holidays in other regions too, though you have to write direct to book.

Denmark: Although there aren't a vast number of farms to choose from, Danish farms are particularly suitable for English families. Most are on Jutland and Funen (home of Hans Christian Andersen so lots to do for kids). The Danish Tourist Board have a brochure (*Holidays in the Country*) that gives full details including whether the farms have animals, and the ages of the farmer's children, so you can match yours with their's. Also one of the farmer's family will speak English. You have your meals with the Danish family who may well cure their own meat, make their own cheese and bake their own bread. Farms often have play areas for children, bikes, riding and fishing nearby. Packages with DFDS (with your own car) or you can fly to Billund or Copenhagen and pick up a hire car with Scanhomes.

France: 2,000 *gîtes* in France are specifically set aside for British visitors and over half of them are on farms, a lot in areas like the Alps where farmers find it more difficult to make ends meet and need the money from tourism. Most are self-catering though a few are b&b. Contact Gîtes de France, 178 Piccadilly, London W1. Tel: 01 491 0914. Or all-inclusive farm holidays offered by Brittany Ferries, Townsend Thoresen, Sealink British Ferries and Sally Line.

Germany: Your accommodation may well be a cottage in the grounds rather than in the main farmhouse. Breakfast and evening meals are also available and you may have use of the farm kitchen. Most of the farms are in southern Germany, in the walking country of the Black Forest, in the fertile Hunsruck region and in and around the vineyards of the Moselle. DER have package tours for a week. You take your own car and can put it part of the way on the train.

Ireland: Irish farmers and their wives are well known for their hospitality. Farms taking in guests (almost 500 of them) are well organised by the Irish Farmhouse Holidays Association who inspect all of them and only include in their guide those who give a friendly welcome. Accommodation may be in seventeenth-century castles, Georgian mansions or modern bungalows with swimming pools. All offer evening meals or high tea, though you can also self-cater. You can expect fresh farm produce, home-baked bread and home-grown vegetables. Sports like fishing and riding may be available nearby. Packages with Aer Lingus, Sealink British Ferries and B&I.

Israel: Kibbutzim are mostly working farms. You stay in guesthouses which are a good deal more comfortable than the accommodation of the residents. You may or may not be able to pull your weight. There will always be children around and plenty going on to keep them busy.

Italy: Agriturism or 'Green Holidays in Italy' has not so far managed to lure many British visitors though the Italians are keen to attract them. Until a year or so ago the farms were listed in a fat book, in Italian, that was virtually impossible to get hold of here. Recently they've produced an abridged booklet (available from the Italian State Tourist Office) in English (though the translations leave a lot to be desired) of farms in different regions, whose owners speak English, though you still have to book through Rome (25% deposit). Farms are dotted all over Italy: among vineyards and olive groves in Tuscany, on sheep farms in Lombardy and Sardinia, in the fruit producing areas of Calabria. Buildings include a medieval castle, a seventeenth-century fortified countryhouse, and a twelfth-century abbey as well as the traditional farmhouse. Most produce their own wine and olive oil, honey, eggs, cheese, fruit, jams and vegetables, which they sell. Many also have pools, nearby riding and fishing. Although many are inland some are within easy reach of the sea. Sometimes meals are provided.

19
CAMPING &
CARAVANNING
HOLIDAYS

All children relish the idea of sleeping under canvas. And these days, you don't have to own as much as a tent peg to do it. Camping is fun and it's cheap.

UK

Camping and caravanning in Britain has changed beyond recognition over the years. Sites are well equipped, many have their own swimming pools, cafés, playgrounds, crazy golf, entertainment, and restaurants, bouncy castles and kids discos. You can choose a site near to a theme park, like the Trentham Gardens caravan site in gardens near Alton Towers (Tel: 0782 657341), or opt for a holiday centre (like Butlin's, Ladbrokes, etc. see holiday centres, p. 112).

If you don't own a caravan there are numerous caravan parks with caravans already on them. The English Tourist Board have made it easier to pick out the good ones by giving 'the best of their kind' a Rose Award. The sites have all been inspected and provide first class holiday caravans in an attractive and well-managed setting. Haven Holidays operate over 30 Holiday Parks and Villages and many of their sites have been awarded the Rose Award. Their family clubs have play areas and playrooms, plus there are Haven Mates who organise a full programme of activities. Sites also have funpools indoors and out. A large number of holiday centres have static caravans on their sites and provide masses to do for children if you want on site organised entertainment.

If you don't own a tent, you can stay in a pre-erected one at two of the Ladbroke Holiday Centres, on the Isle of Wight and in Cornwall. There are caravans too and day and night activities for all the family, including a Starcruiser Club for 4–14 year olds. Details from travel agents. If you do own a tent, see below for where to obtain a list of sites.

Camping and Caravanning Clubs and Guidebooks

If you have your own caravan and want a list of sites in the UK, contact the National Caravan Council; or the Caravan Club operates its own sites.

If you've got your own tent and you'd like information about sites in this country or abroad contact the Camping and Caravan Club or the Automobile Association. For less commercialised sites the Forestry Commission provides caravan and camping sites in natural woodland settings.

The English Tourist Board's *England Holidays* brochure (free from TICs or travel agencies) includes caravan and campsites. Also see their free *Caravan Holiday Parks Rose Award* brochure.

Where to Stay Britain Camping and Caravan Parks (BTA) is available from bookshops or Tourist Information Centres.

Abroad

If you want to camp abroad and you don't have a tent, there are sites all over Europe which come equipped with pre-erected tents. All you have to do is drive up and move in. You'll find them all along the Mediterranean coast, inland in quieter spots like the Dordogne in France, in the Pyrénées in Spain, on farms and on mountainsides in Switzerland, in Germany, Denmark and Austria. Often the tents are in holiday camps with the added bonus of non-stop entertainment and action-packed programmes for children.

The tents come complete with cookers and wardrobes, bedroom areas zipped separately for privacy, sewn-in ground sheets to ensure no creepy crawlies, some even with separate loos, fridges and lights—a far cry from those tiny 'A' frames that were barely big enough to stand up in. And they are pretty hardy to all weather conditions. I should know, I spent a week in one in northern France, I couldn't feel as much as a draught inside during a Force 10 gale! The sites themselves often have a swimming pool and play area, a good shop, perhaps a restaurant, launderette, bar, watersports, adventure playgrounds, trampolines, and . . . children's clubs and supervisors.

On many sites abroad you can stay in a mobile home, a caravilla, chalet or log cabin (mostly Scandinavia). Again you don't have to own it, you just use it rather like an apartment or villa. Many come with fridges and microwaves, freezers and double beds. Sites have the same sort of facilities as the campsites.

You take your own car, although some companies offer fly-

Fun in a French tent.

Caravanning in America's Big Outdoors. Emily, at 2, loved it.

drive, coach or motorail arrangements. The overall holiday price includes the ferry crossing for each adult, the car and the cost of hiring the tent or mobile home. You don't have to stay for the entire time on one site, but can move around and most of the companies will fix *en route* hotels.

Camping and Caravanning Operators

The largest choice of European sites with tents and caravans already on them are bookable through Canvas Holidays, Euro-camp and Sunsites. Sites aren't restricted to the crowded coast-lines, you can find inland sites with fabulous views in remote spots in Scandinavia, Holland or Germany as well as behind beaches in France, Italy, Spain, Portugal and Yugoslavia.

Canvas Holidays started the whole idea off over twenty years ago, but all three companies have unbeatable offers for children. For the last few years they have been offering totally free holidays for children on camping holidays *whenever* you travel, including the school holidays. All you pay for is their insurance. Canvas and Sunsites offer free holidays to under 14's, Eurocamp to under 10's in high season and under 14's at other times. Children get a wide range of extras, from bags and T shirts to maps, 'I Spy' books and diaries. There are also children's couriers on a number of the sites (check they will be at the site you are planning to visit) who organise day-time activities.

Canvas Holidays: Specialise in small groups of tents in attractive settings. Hoopi Club for under 14's. Emphasis on wildlife and conservation, nature trail book, ideas for games, passport and badge. Beginners tents to hire. Add on toilets. Baby patrolling and babysitting. Habitat travel cots. Sports instruction. Trained couriers at selected camps with daily programme of activities.

Eurocamp: Junior Eurocampers Club (kits, diary, route map to colour in), activities run by trained couriers at over 30 sites (treasure hunts, quizzes, cricket matches) morning and after-noon sessions six days a week. Cots, babysitting.

Haven Abroad: Have caravans and tents in France and Spain and also offer free holidays for children under 14 whenever you travel.

Intasun: If your children are over 14 but under 16 you can still qualify for free holidays with Intasun who have a few camp sites in Italy, France, Spain and Yugoslavia. There is an allocation so you have to book early, and the offer is usually restricted to one child per party. Their Carefree Kids Club for 3–12's operates on their site on the Costa Brava and in the south of France.

Sunsites: Magpie Club. 3–13. Large supertents with three bedded children's rooms. Fun packs with things to do on the journey. Trained couriers. Day-time activities for a couple of hours morning and afternoon. Nature walks and picnics. Holiday Superstars competitions (all sports) run in conjunction with Townsend Thoresen for 8–16's at selected sites. Bikes to hire on most sites.

Other companies with mobile homes and good price reductions for children include: Matthews Holidays (France) and, with a long list of countries, Sunsites and Eurocamp, Intasun have mobile homes and the Carefree Kids Club operates on their site in the south of France, and Canvas who have kids clubs with organised activities on a larger number of sites all over Europe, inland and by the sea.

20
HOLIDAY CAMPS, HOLIDAY CLUBS & VILLAGES

Holiday Camps—UK

Early in the 1920's a young Billy Butlin arrived in Britain from Canada with only a fiver in his pocket. He went to work for his uncle in a travelling fun-fair. A few years later he got exclusive rights to import dodgems. Little did he think at the time that he was to start one of the most popular forms of holiday in Britain.

In 1936 Billy Butlin opened Britain's first holiday camp at Skegness; Clacton followed a few years later and holiday camps were in business. By 1948 one in every twenty people who went on holiday went to a holiday camp and 200,000 failed to get in!

By the early sixties holiday camps had to start competing with package tours to foreign parts but they managed to hold their own, offering a brand of fun and entertainment that was unique to Britain. Sir Billy Butlin, knighted in 1964, died in 1980 but the concept has carried on. Butlin's camps (now owned by Rank) are being given a face-lift to the tune of £100 million and companies like Ladbroke, Warner and Pontin's are investing millions in making holiday centres (they don't call them camps any more) all-weather leisure parks designed to be the best family fun you can buy.

These days the old wooden chalets have gone, replaced by de-luxe flats, lodges, bungalows, supertents and caravans, most with their own private bathrooms, carpets, colour tellies and videos, fridges and well-equipped kitchens. If you don't fancy cooking there are on site restaurants, bars and bistros, and if you do, butchers, bakers and supermarkets. Add to that laun-derettes, hairdressers, discos, cabarets, fish and chip shops and a doctor's surgery and you don't really have to venture out of the boundaries. Not that you wouldn't want to. Most holiday centres are in England's top seaside resorts, usually right on the beach!

Children's facilities are second to none: indoor adventure playgrounds with inflatables, ballpools (they swim among ping-pong balls!), sophisticated swimming pools with waterslides, tortuous shutes, wave machines, rapids and waterfalls. Butlin's, Pontin's and Ladbroke run supervised playgrounds and special clubs offering non-stop activities so that you can leave the children to it and go off on your own. The clubs are split into age-groups with appropriate fun, games and activities. There is usually sports tuition by professional players and personalities and big prizes for achievers.

Little babies are taken care of in nurseries with well-equipped play areas. There are cots, highchairs, shallow paddling pools and staff on hand to change nappies and bottle feed. At night babies can be left in the nursery and a baby listening service is available for older children (although this usually only involves someone walking past your chalet and listening out for your child). Holiday camps have always offered babysitting. In the old days at Butlin's they used to put up a sign in the ballroom to call in parents of screaming children that couldn't be quietened by the staff. These days a lot of the kids stay up all night and join in!

While the children are getting on with it there is always plenty going on for parents: gymnastics, football, horse-riding, tennis, darts, billiards and glamorous grannie competitions among them. Sports tuition is by experts and superstars so you really do learn something.

As well as summer holidays, lots of the holiday centres run autumn, spring and winter breaks, often over long weekends. The fully fledged activities for children, though, generally only run during the school holidays. At certain times of year there are weeks devoted to special themes: dancing championships for all ages, sports weeks, gardening, Mother's Day and special family weeks. SPLASH, the association that offers holidays for single parents, buy in weeks at holidays camps, where you will meet other parents in a similar situation.

Ask your travel agent for brochures and look out for special offers, including free rail travel and free places for children right through the season.

Main Operators

Butlin's: Beaver Club for 6–9 year olds, 913 Club for 9–13 year olds. Non-stop programme of fun, sports and adventure, supervised by qualified instructors (including soccer coaching). Night Owl service for leaving babies under 9 months in the nursery. Child listening for older children. Children aged 9 and upwards (including adults) can take part in National Pentathlete awards. Centres at: Bognor, Skegness, Pwllheli, Barry Island, Ayr and

Somerwest World at Minehead. Waterworlds at Bognor, Skegness and Minehead with giant water rides, monsoons and volcanoes, rapids, whirlpools and waterjets. Rail inclusive packages.

Ladbroke Holidays: Sixteen resorts, the Supercentres have the most going on for families. 4−14's can join the Starcruiser Club and get their own space age clubroom. Full entertainment programme with experienced leaders. Lots of prizes, discos, cartoons, trampolines, go karts. Several centres have playgroups, nurseries, nappy washing service, cots and tiny tots play areas and pools. Early evening shows for children. Adventure courses for 10−16's (canoeing, sailing and survival techniques at Carmarthen Bay, south Wales and at Devon valley, Torbay). Holidays are for families and 'bookings from young all male or all female parties will only be accepted at the discretion of the management'.

Pontin's: Twenty-six locations. Crocodile Club and Superteens for 13−15 year olds (competitions with cash prizes). Adventure playgrounds, boating lakes, crazy golf, inflatables and swimming pools. Tennis courts, video games and BMX bikes. Reductions for one parent families. Hobby and leisure courses at certain centres.

Holiday Clubs and Centres Abroad

One way of ensuring you get a good holiday as well as the children is to choose a holiday where there is some sort of organised activity going on. Often you can all do different things without getting under each other's feet and playleaders will relieve you of the children for long patches of the day. Holiday camps, clubs, villages and centres (they all like to be called different things) are an obvious answer, but you do have to put up with other people! Many feature in the pages of tour operators' brochures, available from travel agents.

Some are good old-fashioned holiday camps transported to the sun, complete with cabarets, competitions and entertainers. Others are rather sophisticated (the basic concept is the same but the people who go there are different), and price themselves up a bit. Often the holiday price includes everything: accommodation, all meals, sports and even wine. While it might look expensive in the brochure your final holiday bill will probably be much the same as if you had taken an ordinary half board package tour.

Most holiday clubs run supervised miniclubs for children (see miniclubs, p. 69) so that while they're rushing around having sandcastle competitions, putting on a show or learning to windsurf you can get on with whatever you fancy. Here are a few that might appeal.

Club Med., Greece. Trampolining in the Kid's Club.

Club Med., Tunisia. Afternoon rest time for the little ones.

Holiday Camp, Club, Village Operators

Club Méditerranée: I am a fan of Club Med. A lot of people think that their villages are for swinging singles, that you sleep in straw huts and walk around day and night half naked with beads hanging from your neck. Straw huts went out in the sixties in all but a handful of villages and the vast majority of people who go to Club Med. these days are families with young children. You still pay with beads but since the price includes air fares, transfers, all meals, sports tuition and wine with your dinner, your beads are only needed for cocktails and Cokes. The accommodation is in bungalows or in some cases hotels and the villages are in their own exclusive grounds. There are almost 100 of them, stretching across Europe to North Africa, across to the States, the Caribbean, Bali and Thailand. Most run all year round and there are also villages at ski resorts in France, Italy and Switzerland.

Club Med. have excellent facilities for children and run special clubs, divided into different age-groups at a number of their villages. Children are looked after by trained staff from 9 in the morning until 9 at night. Of course you probably won't want to get rid of your children for all that time every day, but the option is there, and believe me children of all ages very quickly *demand* to go to their club, even if you suggest they stay with you for a bit! At a few villages even babies are looked after in special nurseries—useful even if all you want is someone to be there while they snooze. Activities roll on fast and furious, tennis coaching on mini-courts, a spot of archery or windsurfing before lunch, little crocodiles of kids with rucksacks and sun-hats wending their way down to the beach for games and a ride in boats. Several of the villages also run Circus Schools where, even in a week, children can learn amazing feats and scare the hell out of the parents as they hang upside down from the trapeze or balance on a one wheel bike.

Before I continue to wax lyrical about what the kids can get up to, a few criticisms. Club Meds are French and although there have been attempts over recent years to create what they call International Villages (where English is also widely spoken), basically *les anglais* are usually in the minority and often made to feel that way. I have been to several and when the French arrived and departed (unfortunately on a different day to the English) there were parties and fanfares. When we arrived and departed we had to fit into whatever was happening. When the French went home everything stopped (no sports tuition for example), even though the village still had hundreds of other guests. This affected the children. At one I went to the Circus School was running. Rehearsals were already in progress for the grand show on the last night (where they display all their achievements)—that is the last night of the French contingent. It was the third night for us so, Emily only had time to pick up a few things. Also making friends is more difficult if you arrive when everyone else has made theirs, as international buddies disappear after a day or two. That aside great fun is had by all.

At least one of the playleaders will speak English and younger children quickly form an attachment. Even if there aren't any other English children around (particularly early or late in the season) children seem to find it quite easy to communicate with each other. If you're lucky they may even learn a bit of a foreign language.

The children have their own clubhouse in the grounds: little pegs to hang up clothes, own loos and playgrounds, own pools and playroom. They can turn up when they like and leave when they like (with parents, of course). During the day a sports organiser will extract children who have requested specific activities and after their coaching session return them. They all lunch together and then have a rest. If you want your child to eat with you, you just fish him out.

At around 6 you collect your child and give him a shower and change his clothes. The children meet up for dinner and while you are having yours go off again for evening activities. At around 9 they return to the dining room, a long straggling crocodile, with painted faces, singing, happy and exhausted. Little ones are carried off to bed, exhausted, while older children stay up to watch the cabaret or to have a bit of a dance. There is no specific babysitting, but guards patrol the grounds, so it is safe to leave children sleeping. Two points to watch. If you have a room near the central activities the disco and cabaret will be very loud (it goes on well past midnight), if you have one further away it will be quiet but it will be a long walk to keep checking up on children.

For parents there are non-stop activities all day long, organised with limitless enthusiasm. Sports tuition is first class. If you want to join in you can, if you don't you can sneak away and find a quiet corner to relax in.

Each resort/village is different so check facilities carefully. Some sports are only available to older children. The children are divided by age:

Baby Club: From 4 months to 2 years at selected resorts. Until 6pm. Supervised by qualified staff. Babies restaurant. Qualified nurses on hand. Cots and potties on request. Petit Club at some villages for 2's to 4's.

Mini Club: From, 3, 4, or 6 until 8 depending on village. Qualified instructors. 9am to 9pm including mealtimes. Sports tuition as well as games, handicrafts, shows, Circus School.

Kid's Club: 8–13's. Only operates during French school holidays. Mostly sports tuition. Can come and go as they please.

Juniors' Club: Teenagers. French school holidays. Over and above usual sports, tournaments, picnics, outings.

A Club Méditerranée holiday isn't cheap but it isn't expensive for what you get. There are reductions for children (also applicable if only one adult travels with one child). Book early.

Club Robinson: A village atmosphere in mainland Greece and the islands. The clubs were originally designed for Germans but they now attract an international clientele. Olympic sell them in their holiday brochure. Children's supervisors with daily activities and lots of good facilities.

HCI: Pirate's Club run by experienced aunties for 4 or 5's upwards. Younger children can join in but only with their parents. Clubs open from 9.30 in the morning until 9.30 at night, but the children eat with you. Organised games and outings. Babysitting can be arranged locally. Kids of different nationalities. Hotels and apartments in their own grounds with an international clientele. Mostly Spain, also Greece and Italy, North Africa and Yugoslavia. Summer and winter sun programmes. Also, good reductions for single parents.

Valtur Villages: An Italian style Club Med. (who have a 45 per cent stake in the company) that operates in a very similar way (one price includes all meals, wine, sports tuition and entertainment). A smaller organisation with hotel style rooms, own grounds, good sports facilities. The villages that cater best for children are in southern Italy (also, Corfu, Tunisia, the Ivory Coast and The Maldives). Not cheap (more expensive than Club Med. during the summer but cheaper in the low season). The children's clubs are run like those at Club Med. Children up to 18 are split into different age-groups and looked after from 9 in the morning until 9 at night. Infants from 0−2 in Calabria. Baby Club 2−6 or 3−6 and three other villages in southern Italy. Mini Clubs and Junior Clubs 6−12 and 12−18 in southern Italy and in a mountain resort in the north. Baby food, cots and highchairs available. The predominant language is Italian but at least one member of the staff looking after the children will speak English. Sold in Britain through Serena Holidays.

21

SPORTS,
FAMILY ACTIVITY &
SPECIAL INTEREST
HOLIDAYS

UK

If your children tend to get bored on holiday or they span a variety of ages you may find deciding what to do with them a bit of a problem. Activity and special interest holidays with a theme are an answer. Some of these are based at hotels, others at centres that specialise in the subjects that can inlcude: pony trekking, computers, languages, music, pottery, painting, tennis, sailing or multi-activities. Although you go away as a family, often there is more than one thing going on at the same time, so you can split up and each do something different.

Family Holidays—With a Theme

A lot of sporting or activity holidays are run specifically for families.

The English Tourist Board's *Activity and Hobby Holidays* is probably the best source of information for England. The Scottish Tourist Board have a similar guide called *Adventure and Special Interest Holidays in Scotland*. Accommodation varies; you can stay in universities, some of Britain's top boarding schools, grand country mansions, youth hostels, purpose built centres or hotels. The activities may be on or off the premises. A lot of colleges and universities, for example, run summer courses for families where, as well as specific subjects and supervision for the children, there are often crèches for babies.

Some of the larger hotel chains run hobby and sports holidays too. They are worth investigating outside the summer months too, if you want a long weekend in the spring or autumn. They range from Embassy Hotels Leisure Learning breaks and Dracula weekends run by Quality International to Best Western's sporting breaks and Trusthouse Forte's Special Interest and Activity Breaks where children under 16 can stay free.

For weekend and 'off-season' ideas many activity holidays suitable for families are included in the ETB's *Let's Go*, a guide to short breaks in England (from bookshops). If you want to follow a specific course, The National Institute of Adult Continuing Education produce a booklet listing over 2,000 different residential short courses, taking place in the holidays, including those for families. Some also have crèches. Accommodation is in universities, music schools, study centres and colleges. At a lot of them there are full time nurseries with trained staff to look after babies, children and teenagers. Details from NIACE (England and Wales), 19B De Montfort Street, Leicester. Tel: 0533 551451.

Family Activity Holiday Operators

Below is a selection of just a few of the different types of activity holidays for families, to show you the range of possibilities.

Farmcraft run farmcourses for families (over 5's), with tuition in making butter, milking cows, keeping bees, goats and pigs. Accommodation is in an old farmbuilding, self-catering. Shipley Country Park, Heanor, Derbyshire. Tel: 0602 305611.

Hobby & Leisure Holidays offer about 100 sport and leisure activities at Pontin's Holiday Centres and Waterside Caravan Parks throughout the UK. Not just sports, but also family leisure weeks (huge range of subjects including cooking for children, making kites, jewellery and enamel work, etc.).

HF Holidays have designated walking weeks (under 5's free) at several of their holiday centres (large houses) that are specially geared for families. Adults and children join organised walks but for those with little legs there's a crèche so that parents can go off on their own. Also provided are cots, highchairs, buggies, a laundry and somewhere to buy babyfood and nappies. Also half-term family holidays. Destinations include several lochs in Scotland, Scarborough (Kinderland is their big attraction), Swanage, Thurlstone Sands in Devon, the Isle of Wight, Conwy in Wales, Alnmouth in Northumbria and Conistonwater in the Lake District. HF also run special interest and hobby holidays for families in subjects like scrabble, cycling and pony trekking.

Horse-drawn Caravans: Take it easy through the side roads in Norfolk, Yorkshire, Isle of Wight or Wales, through Waveney Valley Horse Holidays (Airstation Farm, Pulham St Mary, Diss, Norfolk. Tel: 0379 741228), North Yorkshire Romany Holidays (Lilac Cottage, Great Thirkleby, Thirsk. Tel: 0845 401486), Wight

Horsedrawn Caravans Holidays (White Horse Road, Porchfield, Newport, Isle of Wight. Tel: 0983 525467), Welsh Horse-drawn Holidays (Rhyd-y-Bont Farm, Talgarth. Tel: 0874 711346).

Loughborough University Summer Programme: Wide range of courses. Residential or non-residential. Whatever subject you choose there is a crèche and separate playgroup for under 5's with indoor and outdoor acitivities, cots and refreshments provided. Youth group for 5–12's: competitions, sports, riding, gymnastics, etc. and local excursions (ratio staff to kids 1:10). Special Horizon courses for 13–17's (cycling, microcomputing, etc.). Centre for Extension Studies, University of Technology, Loughborough. Tel: 0509 267494.

There are other universities with similar programmes (see National Institute book as above, or the ETB's *Activity and Hobby Holidays*).

Marlborough College in Wiltshire (Tel: 0672 53888) has multi-activity holiday courses for children (from 7 upwards) to take part in while you are doing another subject.

Millfield School in Street, Somerset, is an exclusive boarding school in magnificent grounds. In the summer holidays they offer well over 360 courses (and keep on half the term-time staff to run them). The 130 acres of grounds have five sports halls, and three golf courses. The kids can do lots of different things (or multi-activity) while you stick to a couple of main subjects. Attend daily or stay in family rooms or you can send the children off to share with other children in 'houses' in the village. Crèche, evening activities. They also take kids on their own from 8.

PGL Family Adventure Holidays take place in boarding schools and colleges. Some family rooms, also dormitories. All sorts of sports, handicrafts, computers and multi-activities. Playschemes for 4–6 year olds. England and Wales.

Alternatively, you can make sure you find something interesting to do once you get to your holiday destination. The Scottish Tourist Board, for example, publish *See Scotland at Work* that includes a wide range of places to visit from whisky distilleries to woollen mills, silversmiths to candle makers, plus craft courses to go on. The AA publish *Craft Workshops in the English Countryside*, produced in conjunction with CoSIRA. Or look up the address of the regional tourist board in the area you are planning to visit and they will send you details of courses and activities in their region.

Abroad

A quick glance at tour operators' brochures will tell you that there are a lot of hotel/self-catering complexes abroad that specialise in sports with tuition for children as well as adults.

Here are a few who offer special interest or sporting holidays abroad that are suitable for children and parents.

Family Activity Holiday Operators

American Round-Up: Holidays on dude ranches in the States. Horseback riding, camping out, river rafting, rodeos. Lots of ranches to choose from, some have full time counsellors supervising children's programmes (see also USA under Country by Country, p. 67).

Anglo-Dutch Sports: Cycling in Holland. Specific tours and routes. Hire a bike or take your own. Can also put your bikes on the train as you go along. They book hotels and ferry crossings.

Crystal Holidays: Specialise in sporting holidays in Austria. Several holiday villages with a wide range of sports: summer snow skiing, tennis, riding, cycling, etc. Resorts have masses going on. Good reductions for children. Some hotels have playrooms, many have pools.

PGL: Family Adventure programme in Europe: self-catering and sailing on the Languedoc coast of France (bungalows, tents, minimum age 7); canoeing on the Swedish lakes (studios, chalets, minimum age 9); cycling in Holland (family hotel), about 30 miles a day (minimum age 11); or hiking and multi-activities in the Austrian Tyrol (chalet style pension, minimum age 9). Travel by ferry with your own car to Sweden and France (under 4's free). Good reductions for older children. By air or car to Austria, by coach and ferry to Holland. Also Family Skiing in winter in Austria with a kindergarten for 'dry' children.

22
HOLIDAYS FOR UNACCOMPANIED CHILDREN

UK

'School makes you feel funny inside if you don't get a sum right. This makes you feel all happy.' (Tracy, 7, Dolphin Holidays)

Most unaccompanied children's holidays take place in schools or colleges 'rented' out for the school holidays; but that's where the resemblance ends.

'You don't go around calling the teachers Sir, you call them by their first names.'

Whether you choose to send your child to a residential camp or to a day centre, he'll be offered a wide range of activities, some of them potentially dangerous: canoeing, sailing, riding, climbing, orienteering, riding mini motorbikes and abseiling among them. Some centres offer a bit of everything, multi-activities, which include sports as well as subjects like arts and crafts, computers, video film making and fashion design. But even if your child is only going to do the odd few hours of canoeing you'll want reassurance that the staff are qualified and that the safety standards are high. Some centres concentrate on a particular sport and are approved by the relevant sporting authority (Royal Yachting Association, British Canoe Union, etc.). But most of those offering general or multi-activities aren't (though the premises, if it is a school, will be). As a general rule you would be wise not to send your children anywhere that doesn't insist on their wearing hard hats for riding and life jackets for all water sports, and that doesn't insist they should be able to swim at least 50 yards for water-based activities.

You should look through brochures carefully to see just what goes on in a typical day and pick a centre that suits your child's interests and personality. There is no point in sending a child who hates the water, canoeing, or a boisterous ten year old who never sits still to do arts and crafts. Pick subjects your child is interested in or, better still, show him the brochures and discuss it all between you.

Day Camps

'We do hard work at school, and easy work here.'
(Georgie, 4)

Sending children off on their own on holiday for the first time can be a traumatic experience for both you and them. So letting them get the feel of it by opting for a day camp is a good idea. Many of the day camps take 3–5 year olds as well as older children. Should you be anxious that your small child wouldn't be able to stand the pace, nor do without his afternoon snooze, most build in a quiet rest time after lunch. The Camp Director at a Dolphin Camp for teenies told me he'd only ever seen one child fall asleep before going home time!

All day camps offer a multi-activity programme which means they can dabble in a bit of everything. Some of the brochures list up to 60 different subjects, which makes it a bit difficult for some children to choose. Often sports, like riding or mini motorbikes, cost extra. Do not let your child get too excited about a specific subject. If the camp are having a quiet week, with fewer children, some of the subjects may be cancelled. On the other hand, it isn't the end of the world if your child has chosen certain subjects and then fancies doing something else, many centres are flexible and will allow them to switch subjects. He may, of course, not get a choice. Some camps, although they have a range of subjects, stick to a timetable, so the children get a chance to try a bit of everything. It is worth encouraging your child to try something he wouldn't get a chance to do anywhere else, like video film making, archery or capsizing a canoe in the swimming pool. Nearly all the kids opt for swimming, and a lot for computer games. Although the subjects are taken seriously the children enjoy themselves. Sometimes they can cram as many as six or seven into a day. Since it is their holiday, and quite a test of independence, you might as well let them get on with it.

Your child's school may know about a reputable day camp in your area. Once you find an operator you can ask them for the names and addresses of parents who have sent their children before and then ask the parents if they would recommend it. You can also usually have a look for yourself if it is a day camp

Face painting at a Dolphin Day Camp for teenies.

near your home and your child isn't planning to go on the first day of operation. Most of them operate in the Easter and summer school holidays. Reputable day camp operators include: Camp Beaumont, Dolphin and PGL.

Residential Camps

'I haven't been bored for a whole week.'
(Steven, 11, Glasgow)

Week and longer residential camps operate up and down the country. Some take children as young as 5, others from 7. Since some of the day camps are also fully-fledged residential centres, children who start off this way can see what it would be like to stay (when they get braver). PGL, who have been running unaccompanied children's holidays for thirty years, take many thousands of kids away each year. Lots of children get homesick on the first day but it doesn't take long for them to get over it and 'less than a handful' insist on packing it all in and going home early.

Not all centres offer 'multi-activities', although these are certainly best for younger children and those who can't make their minds up about what they'd like to do. Some centres specialise in specific sports, like riding, sailing, climbing or football. Equipment is usually provided and coaching is often by famous sports personalities and professionals. You can tell how 'serious' it is by the number of hours a day the children are expected to indulge in the particular sport. PGL, for example, run soccer, cricket, fishing, tennis, riding and canoeing courses as well as general multi-activities. Dolphin and Camp Beaumont also run specialist sports weeks with expert tuition. And children on multi-activity courses can pay a bit extra for other sports like mini-motorbikes or riding.

In the evening when most of the children are pretty tired there are barbecues, treasure hunts, videos, discos, competitions etc. before hot chocolate and bed. Bathing is often up to them, although there are also 'official' bath nights for slackers.

The children often sleep in dormitories (segregated by age and sex). If you are sending younger children you might like to ask if a 'teacher', or 'monitor' as they are often called, sleeps in the dorm with them. Brothers and sisters may not be able to sleep together. Bedtimes are staggered and fixed according to age. There are inevitable pillow fights and much giggling after lights out.

Food is not gourmet. School-type dinners are the norm though few kids complain. You can usually request vegetarian meals. In between there's the tuckshop. Some are open all day long, others for a short time each day. If you want to discourage your child from stuffing his face full of crisps and chocolate all day, don't give him much money to spend. Some of the camps restrict the amount of pocket money anyway.

You should label all your children's clothes carefully. Almost all of them manage to lose something. A large proportion of kids come home in what you sent them in, without so much as even unpacking the rest. Do not send any 'best' clothes. They will not be dressing for dinner, although something for the disco may be necessary. All they really need is shorts and T shirts, a track suit and water proofs, strong trainers, swimming gear, nightwear and something to 'bop' in.

In case of illness or accidents there is usually a Matron or nurse, resident or living nearby. Minor scrapes are inevitable. There is usually a phone box if you want them to ring home (don't be surprised if they forget). If you want them to write give them a stamped addressed envelope. Once hooked, most kids want to go again.

SPLASH, the association for one parent holidays, also arrange holidays for unaccompanied children (see p. 133).

More Questions to Ask

* Is escorted travel provided?
* Do they insist on your child being able to swim 50yds for water-based activities. Do they provide hard hats (riding) and life vests?
* How many hours a day are spent doing specific sports?
* What are the qualifications of the staff?
* Is the centre approved by the appropriate authority?
* What is the ratio of staff to kids?

You may not get answers to all of these questions but from their

Bikin', shootin' and fishin'. Multi-activities mean a bit of everything.

reaction you can decide for yourself if you think the place is suitable.

Best Sources of Information

The English Tourist Board's *Activity and Hobby Holidays* and the Scottish Tourist Board's *Adventure and Special Interest Holidays in Scotland*, list details of all the camps offering multi-activity and special interest holidays.

Abroad

Sending your child abroad on his own needs a little more courage (and the same sorts of questions answered as you'd expect from a camp here). You may not consider it worth it if the programme doesn't actually include much of the foreign place and the children spend all their time wthin the confines of the centre itself.

Holiday Operators: Abroad

Dolphin have a Mediterranean Magic experience in the south of France for 12–18 year olds in summer, with canoeing down the Ardèche and sailing; they sleep in tents. Dolphin also take 12–17 year olds skiing in France in winter.

PGL take 13–15's on a barge holiday in Holland, canoeing, sailing and windsurfing in the South of France, and skiing in Austria and Andorra.

23
WORKING HOLIDAYS

Working holidays aren't really holidays, they are more like hard work and are rarely suitable for children under 16. You should explain to your child that it is not just a way of travelling cheaply; volunteers are expected to pull their weight and can't expect home comforts. Needless to say much fun is had by all, provided they know what they are letting themselves in for.

The best source of working holidays available, both in this country and abroad, is *Working Holidays*, published by the government-backed Central Bureau for Educational Visits and Exchanges (from bookshops). The book explains about permits and visas and is jam packed with ideas of jobs available throughout the world. The possibilities are endless from au pairing in France to being a tour operator's rep. on a campsite, your child could volunteer to protect Osprey eggs in Scotland, build a barn in Denmark or to act as a 'helper' on holidays for disabled children. A word of warning from the Central Bureau though to young people who want to 'do good':

> 'Many people don't have the slightest idea of how harrowing it can be working with old or handicapped people. Not only do you have to be physically strong but mentally strong too.'

Although there are holiday jobs available for younger children, particularly in conservation in this country, where several organisations take children from 12 upwards, mostly children have to be over 16 or 18. On the whole most firms offering jobs are reputable but there have been more than a few instances of fly-by-night operators (notoriously offering non-existent grape-picking holidays in France). However, if your child finds a job through the Bureau's guide it should be reliable as they vet companies they include carefully and only list operators who have been operating successfully for at least three years.

The most popular holiday according to the Bureau is being an au pair 'to a rich aristocratic family in Italy who go off to the sea or the Lakes for the summer'. Next comes grape picking, followed by 'getting down to the South of France and picking up a job selling ice-cream and doughnuts'.

Perhaps not the sort of thing you fancy your 16 year old doing.

UK

Conservation holidays are perhaps the most suitable. Volunteers are taken from about the age of 16 upwards and they are offered projects which could be anything from clearing litter on South Coast beaches or helping to maintain a narrow gauge railway to conserving and repairing some of Britain's cathedrals.

The following organisations have jobs for young people.

Acorn Camps: The National Trust run a variety of conservation holidays for over 16's. For a week at a time a dozen or so volunteers tackle projects like fencing, woodland clearance and planting, sand dune stabilisation and footpath maintenance. Teams could be sent to repair the much trampled-on Pennine Way, build dry stone walls in Wales or dig out a lagoon in the Fens to encourage wildfowl. Some of the camps are centred on Corfe Castle in Dorset; you stay in converted farmhouses or village halls. Minimal charge to cover board and lodging. Evenings are free. Details from the National Trust, PO Box 12, Westbury, Wiltshire. Tel: 0373 826302. Send large sae.

Thistle Camps: The National Trust for Scotland run similar projects for over 16's. Details from 5 Charlotte Square, Edinburgh. Tel: 031 226 5922.

British Trust for Conservation Volunteers run conservation projects on nature reserves, in National Parks and on National Trust properties. Age 16 upwards. On weekends local groups may accept children from 12 upwards. Instruction is given on the use of tools and equipment, traditional techniques and other conservation skills. Also talks and guided tours. Some holidays are more arduous than others and volunteers must be physically and mentally equipped to cope with working on remote and exposed sites. Details from the Administrator, 36 St Mary's Street, Wallingford, Oxford. Tel: Wallingford 39766.

Abroad

Interviews and selections for jobs abroad are usually by letter and, as with most jobs, your child will have to convince the employer that he or she really wants it, and not just the money (even though there's not much of it). It helps to send a CV, a couple of references, and an sae. The children should tell them when they are free. For most jobs abroad, students are expected to pay their own way there and back (for summer camps in the States, a ticket may be forwarded but the cost will be deducted from the wages). The Central Bureau's *Working Holidays* covers countries worldwide and numerous possibilities. Over 16's can: excavate and restore archaeological sites in Italy, research and excavate an ancient agricultural settlement in the Judean Hills in Israel, or help pick grapes in Germany. For excavation jobs applicants are often expected to have had some sort of experience, perhaps doing a similar thing in this country.

Most of the jobs offered to young people are during the summer holidays but students are more likely to be accepted if they can start earlier than normal end of term time.

Workcamps abroad normally have exchange agreements with partner organisations in this country so it is rarely necessary for students to have to write direct.

Before you let your child off on a working holiday abroad you should try and persuade him or her to do one in this country first, especially if they have never lived away from home before. It might also be an idea to do it with a friend. Before committing themselves students should ask: how much free time they can expect to get, are meals provided or will they have to cook for themselves, will they need a sleeping bag, how the wages are paid, and will it cost them anything?

24
SINGLE
PARENT
HOLIDAYS

For many single parents the thought of holidaying alone with their children is a pretty daunting one. The main problem for most single parents is finance, followed by loneliness. It is simply not much fun holidaying alone with children if everybody else seems to be in couples. Finding a holiday company that doesn't discriminate (in its price structure) against one parent holidaying with one or more children is difficult—most of them only offer reductions for children travelling with two full fare paying adults. Finding a holiday where there will be other people on their own is even harder. It is often easier to find good reductions for winter holidays than it is in the summer.

SPLASH is the only organisation of any size that is specifically set up to cater for holidays for single parents. Run as a charity, SPLASH was originally affiliated to Gingerbread Holidays and is now on its own. They basically buy in selected weeks from tour operators and holiday companies and sell them at a discount to single parents. The type of holiday is varied, from holiday centres (Warner, Butlin's and Pontin's) to apartments in Florida. They attract a wide range of single parents from different walks of life, take, inevitably, more women than men, and point out that 'a parent can be single even if they have a partner if they have to holiday alone for whatever reason'. The women and men who travel with them may be widowed, separated or divorced. Their husbands could be in prison, have jobs abroad or be in the armed forces. All they need have in common is that they are holidaying on their own with the kids. If you travel with SPLASH you will be at an ordinary package tour hotel or apartment but you can be sure that there will be other single parents on the same trip.

SPLASH have also recently introduced the concept of an exchange system for families and/or children, in co-operation with single parent groups abroad, including Parents without Partners in the States. The idea is that you and your child or children can be put in touch with a single parent family abroad and would be invited to stay, reciprocating in your own home later in that year. Obviously you have to have room to put up a visiting family.

It is also possible for your child or children to go off on their own, giving you a break and the parent overseas a similar one when you invite his or her child back.

SPLASH also run a few holidays for unaccompanied children. Although there are numerous holiday companies running this sort of holiday it is quite a good idea if your children don't often meet other children in the same situation as themselves for them to holiday together. For a child of single parents it could be very important indeed for him to see there are lots of other kids in the same boat.

SPLASH offer the following holidays: holiday centres in England and Wales (Butlin's, Warner, Pontin's); camping and caravanning in France, Italy, Portugal, Corfu and Spain; un-accompanied children; activities; canal cruising; and farm holidays in England. Also Christmas breaks.

You may not want to go on holiday solely with other single parents, although most single parents would probably be happier if there were some people on their own with their children. One of the ways of meeting other people is to choose a holiday where there is a lot going on. In this country have a look in the English Tourist Board's *Hobby and Activity Holidays* (see p. 119), or choose a holiday centre (see p. 113) like Butlin's, a company like PGL Family Adventure (UK and abroad), or Club Méditerranée or HCI for holidays abroad. A large number of people go on their own or with friends on this sort of holiday, so you won't be faced with a barrage of couples. You are encouraged to mix and be friendly both by the enormous number of activities going on, day and night and because the children are taken care of in supervised miniclubs. It is quite easy to get talking to other parents when you drop your kids off in the morning.

Package Tours

If you want to go on an ordinary package tour you have to shop around very carefully for reductions that apply to only one adult travelling with one or more children. From year to year package holiday operators make gestures to offer holidays with good reductions for single parents. Often these are limited in number and only apply to travel outside the school holidays, making them virtually useless if you have school-age children. The best deals are during the winter, to self-catering apartments and on autumn or spring breaks. Most hotel based package tours abroad attract two parent families, but on holidays where reductions are offered to single parents you may well find a few people in the same situation as yourself.

Price Reductions for Single Parents

The following tour operators, holiday companies and hotel chains offer price reductions for single parents travelling with one or more children. Offers are usually limited to a certain resort and hotel or to specific weeks in the year.

HCI: Reductions for single parents at selected clubs abroad. All year round. Numerous activities and supervised miniclubs.

Matthews specialise in rather classy mobile homes on campsites in France. Their holidays are for families, two children under 14 can travel free with one parent, regardless of season.

Hotel Chains: In the UK—Trusthouse Forte, Superbreak Mini Holidays.
Abroad—Sol Hotels own a large number of hotels in Spain and the Balaerics; they feature in major tour operators' brochures. Reductions and free places for children travelling with only one parent as well as playrooms, miniclubs, activities, etc.

Tour Operators: Thomson, Global, Horizon, Intasun, Lancaster Family First, Yugotours, Sunmed, Enterprise, Sovereign, Austro Tours (skiing Austria), are among those with a rather more generous attitude to single parents.

25
HOLIDAYS FOR HANDICAPPED CHILDREN

If you have a disabled child and holidays have not been satisfactory in the past for you, there are organisations and holiday companies that can help.

You can get a full list of organisations who provide holidays for disadvantaged children from the Holiday Care Service (see below). They collate material on holidays for those with special needs and have details about travel and holidays both in this country and abroad. They will also direct you to organisations that can offer financial assistance and have files full of information that ranges from hotels that cater for special diets and hire car companies that take wheelchairs to museums with special arrangements for visitors with impaired hearing or vision.

Guidebooks

The English Tourist Board's *Activity and Hobby Holidays* lists centres that cater for disabled children and will instruct them in all sorts of sporting activities. Other useful guides include the Wales Tourist Board's booklet on *Holidays for the Disabled* and the AA's *Travellers Guide for the Disabled* which details access and facilities in inspected accommodation, campsites, places to visit and motorway service areas, as well as toilets. It also covers accommodation abroad on touring itineraries.

When you are choosing a place to stay, whether it is a holiday centre or hotel, you will have to check very carefully on the facilities available, particularly if your child is in a wheelchair.

You should not rely, necessarily, on general hotel guides that include a wheelchair symbol, along with the number of private bathrooms and whether they take credit cards. Although most hotel and restaurant guides do attempt to help disabled visitors, few will have been inspected to ensure that in practice they are suitable for people with impaired mobility. You should contact the hotel or holiday company direct and specify your particular needs. If there are no ground floor rooms available in a hotel, for example, and there is a lift, check that it is big enough to take the wheelchair and that there are no further steps to negotiate to your bedroom.

Going Abroad

If you are planning a trip abroad by air check with the airline you are travelling with about what they can do for you. You can get a free brochure *Care in the Air* from the Air Transport Users Committee, 129 Kingsway, London WC2. To find out about the facilities for disabled travellers at individual UK airports write to the British Airports Authority, Publications Office, Gatwick Airport, Gatwick, West Sussex. For travel further afield *Access Travel: Airports* is published by the US Dept of Transportation and gives details of facilities and services at several hundred airports worldwide. Write to Access America, Washington, DC 20202, USA. Try and find out before you travel just what the arrangements are for boarding and checking in to save anxiety when you get there.

Wherever you are going and by whatever means of transport make sure *everyone* knows about your special requirements. If your travel agent has made all the arrangements for you, make a few phone calls yourself, direct to hotels or the airline you are travelling with to confirm arrangements.

Organisations and Holiday Companies

Here are a few, but by no means all, organisations that will give you further information about holidays for disabled or disadvantaged children or arrange them themselves.

Association for All Speech Impaired Children, 347 Central Markets, Smithfield, London EC1. Tel: 01 236 3632. The association's concern is with children who have language problems, but who are otherwise physically normal. Activity weeks organised with children broken down into age-groups, from 5 upwards. Each child has a young adult trained volunteer who accompanies him: canoeing, sailing, climbing, etc. Also music, and arts and crafts.

BREAK, 20 Hooks Hill Road, Sheringham, Norfolk. Tel: 0263 823170. A charitable trust set up in 1968 to provide holidays for handicapped children and give their families a break from the constant demands of looking after them. Parents are welcome but the Centres are organised around the needs of handicapped guests. Family weeks are run from time to time. Three houses on the Norfolk coast run as family homes. Pools, wide range of activities on site as well as outings, horseriding, and visits to the sea. Maladjusted, deprived or disturbed children up to 16.

The Calvert Trust Adventure Centre, Little Crosthwaite, Underskiddaw, Keswick, Cumbria. Tel: 0596 72254. Multi-activity adventure courses for over 12's and their helpers: sailing, canoeing, swimming, riding, birdwatching, etc. Tuition in all activities.

Holiday Care Service, 2 Old Bank Chambers, Station Road, Horley, Surrey. Tel: 0293 774535. Will provide list of companies and organisations involved in the provision of holidays in the UK for disabled and disadvantages children and young people. Will also help with practical advice on all aspects of travel.

The Jane Hodge Home, 55b Merthyr Road, Whitchurch, Cardiff. Tel: 0222 613304. Charity subsiding holidays for handicapped children with a home near Cowbridge.

National Deaf Children's Society, 45 Hereford Road, London W2. Tel: 01 229 9272. Send sae for annual *Holiday Possibilities for Deaf Children* which gives ideas for holidays for children on their own or with adults. Wide range of activities, including sports.

Riding for the Disabled Association, Avenue 'R', National Agricultural Centre, Kenilworth, Warwickshire. Tel: 0203 56107. Local groups arrange riding holidays. Children who cannot walk can often happily ride and many mentally handicapped children also enjoy horseriding.

The Royal Association for Disability and Rehabilitation, 25 Mortimer Street, London W1. Tel: 01 637 5400. RADAR publish several useful books including a fat *Holidays for Disabled People* that includes voluntary organisations that arrange holidays for disabled children and places that will take unaccompanied children. Available in W.H. Smith or send £2. They also publish *Holiday Accommodation for Children and Young People* (free).

Royal Society for Mentally Handicapped Children and Adults, 123 Golden Lane, London EC1. Tel: 01 253 9433. MENCAP published the *Holiday Accommodation Guide* (£1 plus 25p postage) with details of where mentally handicapped are welcomed either on their own or with their families. MENCAP Holiday Services, 119 Drake Street, Rochdale, Lancashire will send you details (sae) of the holidays they arrange throughout the UK for children whose handicaps are not normally catered for.

Spastics Society, 16 Fitzroy Square, London W1. Tel: 01 387 9571. General holiday facilities leaflets, including adventure holidays for handicapped children and young adults. They have a holiday adviser and run their own field study centre in Cornwall where children can learn to swim, sail, canoe, fish and abseil.

Sweden: The Swedish National Tourist Office produce a detailed guide for the physically handicapped, blind, and hard of hearing traveller as well as allergy sufferers (the Scandic Hotel Chain have allergy free rooms). Recent legislation in Sweden states that all public buildings must be accessible to the disabled, even the Stockholm tube system is equipped with facilities for the handicapped, and many Swedish hotels have rooms specifically designed for them. The brochure is in English, and gives information about four holiday homes run by the Swedish National Association for the Handicapped as well as information on air and bus services (there is a special transport system—Fardtjanst—for the disabled). Several holiday areas have developed sports facilities for the disabled and suitable accommodation in hotels, chalet and campsites is also detailed.

Threshold Travel, Wrendal House, 2 Whitworth Street West, Manchester. Tel: 061 236 9763. The largest tour operator in the UK specialising in holidays worldwide for the physically disabled. All aspects of the holidays in their brochure are suitable for the disabled (including transfers to the resort in specially adapted mini-buses or cars). They cater for the physically handicapped traveller wanting to take a conventional holiday with family or friends. Hotels and resorts are inspected. Holidays range from Kenya safaris to visits to DisneyWorld in Florida. Group tours, hotels, self-catering, boating holidays in the UK, etc. No specific holidays just for children but reductions for 2–11's.

Part Three

TRAVELLING, PRACTICAL ADVICE & INFORMATION

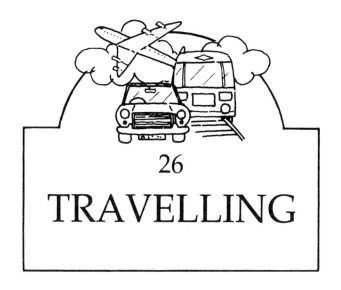

26

TRAVELLING

Travelling by Air

Try and choose a flight that leaves at a sensible time of day, wherever possible. Sometimes, if you are travelling with a tour operator, the brochure doesn't always make it clear as to what time the plane leaves. If in doubt, ring the tour operator direct before you make a booking. Night flights are very disruptive if you're travelling with young children and you may well find another tour operator going to the same place with a flight at a more civilised time. A very early start is far, far, better than a very late one.

Some airlines are a lot better than others at making families feel more comfortable, particularly if you are planning to travel long distance. Some are understanding about mothers wanting to breastfeed on board, others still, amazingly, discourage it; some provide nappies and babyfood, skycots and games, others nothing at all. And airports themselves vary, both in this country and at the other end.

You will not usually get any special facilities for your children on a charter flight—that is a flight booked through a tour operator for which you are paying an all-inclusive price. You'll be lucky if there's even a spare seat. Once on board, if you see that there is space and you have a baby or toddler on your lap, you may be able to move into it. Ask the stewardess after take off, when the seat belt signs have been switched off. If you do take your own jars or bottles on board, label them carefully to avoid confusion. For older children, mealtimes will not necessarily coincide with their hunger, nor satisfy it necessarily if they do; it

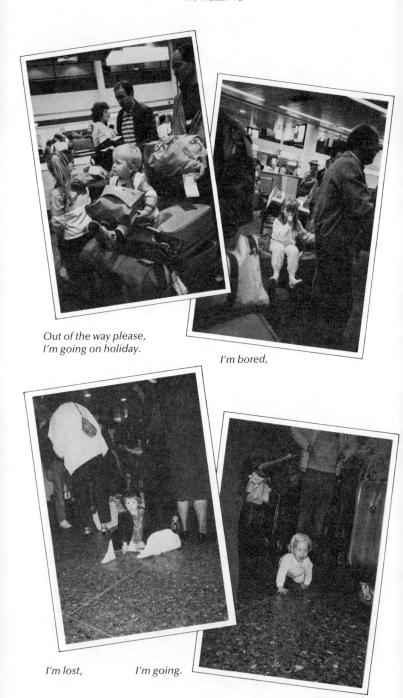

*Out of the way please,
I'm going on holiday.*

I'm bored,

I'm lost,   *I'm going.*

is worth taking your own picnic. Don't bother with drink, it is bulky, and you can always get juice or squash.

Airfares

In general, infants under 2 are charged 10 per cent of the adult fare on scheduled flights abroad (one infant for each fare paying passenger, including accompanying children over 12) and under 12's qualify for a reduction of 50 per cent. Children over 12 pay full fare. Under 2's do not qualify for their own seats. On UK domestic flights, infants under 3 travel free (on your lap). Cheap Superpex fares do not allow child discounts, although Apex and Pex fares allow children 50 per cent reductions. Cheaper, long-haul flights charge children 67 per cent of the adult fare. Airfare prices are quite complex, so you will need to check with the individual airlines.

The cheapest way of taking a child abroad is on an all-inclusive package tour using a charter flight. Individual companies charge children varying amounts. Infants under 2 often go free (or are charged a nominal amount). Under 12's usually get discounts, although some tour operators (particularly to self-catering properties in European destinations) also give good discounts for children up to 16 and over.

Airports

Airports can be a nightmare if you are travelling with a young family at the peak of the season. All you can do is be prepared for the worst and you might be pleasantly surprised.

Most UK airports (and larger international airports at the other end) have a special mother and baby room where you can change and feed your baby. In them you'll find toilets, sinks and space to change nappies. Sometimes you get a chair or two, a kettle and a bottle warmer. Occasionally there might be a play-pen or a box of tissues. Most do not have supplies, but they do offer privacy and peace away from the hustle and bustle of the airport. Sometimes the mother and baby room will be locked or pitch dark. I once nearly dropped Emily out of the carrycot trying to find a light switch (I think it was in Ireland). If you do find it's locked, go to the Information Desk. They will give you the key!

Airport Entertainment

Most UK airports have a spectators' enclosure or gallery for children to watch planes taking off and arriving. There may be some ubiquitous computer games, or try the destination game. Pack a small map of Europe or the world (the sort you get in the in-flight magazines). Stick the kids in front of the arrivals and departures board and get them to find the places on the map. Terminal 4 at Heathrow has a crèche (open from 7am–10pm) where up to 35 children from 2–8, labelled with tickets matching their boarding cards, can play under the care of four trained nurses. The crèche is equipped with books, games, puzzles and dolls, and there is a climbing frame, bikes and pedal cars to burn off excess energy. Heathrow also has an unsupervised Play Area in the Roof Garden on top of the Queen's Building, with swings, slides and climbing frames. There is a small entrance charge.

Airport Meals

Eating always plays an important part in keeping children occupied. But do not feed them rich or greasy foods however hungry they say they are if you want to avoid them throwing up. Restaurants at most airports serve breakfast if you left home in a hurry (including mini packs of cereals). At Heathrow the self-service restaurants in Terminals 1 and 3 are open 24hrs a day. Shortstop at Gatwick provides hamburgers around the clock and a 31 flavour ice-cream parlour, and at both Gatwick and Heathrow you can get freshly squeezed orange juice. Algy's Diner at Edinburgh airport is decorated with souvenirs from old aircraft should you have an interested child.

Airport Shops

As well as duty-frees, most UK holiday airports sell paperbacks, books on travelling, comics, sunscreens, and sweets. Long-lasting sucking sweets certainly help 'unpop' ears for take-off and landing, but do not be tempted to take chocolate bars on journeys to hot places. Shops also sell film (strangely not often the cassettes for 126 instamatics), and toys and games, including teddy bears: Harry Heathrow, Gary Gatwick, Eddie Edinburgh, Stanley Stanstead, Gordon Glasgow, Archie Aberdeen and Percy Prestwick among them. There are usually shops and sometimes a restaurant in the departure lounge on the other side of Passport Control. It's worth waiting to buy books there as often they are advance copies that haven't yet hit the high street bookshops.

At the Other End

Foreign airports vary considerably, from one room shacks to International airports with the same sort of facilities as Heathrow or Gatwick. Although you might want to get out of it as quickly as possible on arrival it is worth having a look around to see what you'll get on the way home. Loos and restaurants in small foreign airports are only available before you go through passport control. If there is no restaurant or bar selling food, pack supplies of food and drink for delays on the homeward journey. If you are travelling independently, telephone the airport before you set off on the way home to confirm your seat. If you are on a package, check with your representative if the return flight is due to leave on time.

The Journey

Be prepared for delays, both ends, and pack hand luggage

Gary Gatwick and Emily.

Families usually board first.

accordingly. Children of all ages should be given a rucksack in which to keep their favourite toy, 'cuddly' or teddy bear (do not pack it in your luggage), a supply of bribes (yes, you can have another sweet if you stop asking when we're going to get there) and, depending upon their age, something to keep them occupied (activity book, small computer game, anything that's self-contained and time consuming).

Always pack enough food and drink for delays at the airport, for on the plane and for the journey at the other end. And always take at least one change of clothing for the baby; there's nothing worse than travelling with a damp baby on your lap, whose clean clothes are stuck at the bottom of your suitcase.

All Aboard

Families with young children may be asked to board first. This is sometimes an airline policy, although with others it is on request only. Ask when your gate number is called or when you get to your special departure area. Hang on to the baby buggy. Most airlines will let you take it as far as the steps of the plane. They will then take it away and either put it in the cabin or the hold. Just before you are due to land ask a stewardess for it back. If it is in the hold you should wait at the foot of the steps until they get it for you. Insist you have it immediately (rather than let them send it with your luggage) as the walk to Customs and the wait for your suitcases might be a long one.

If you have a child who is interested in seeing the pilot's cabin, you can ask a stewardess during the flight. This is usually possible. But choose your time carefully. Don't ask just when meals or duty-frees are being dished out.

Breastfeeding

'We do not approve of breastfeeding in public.' (Caribbean Airways)

Most airlines (charter and scheduled) accept that nursing mothers have to feed their babies on planes, and are sympathetic to their doing it and to requests for privacy. Some will allocate nursing mothers bulkhead seats, or they might let you sit in the curtained off crew area to feed your baby, provided the plane has one. It should not be necessary for you to do it in the loo! Sometimes it is up to the individual crew, although most airlines do have a policy about it. Of the thirty or so major airlines I contacted, the following weren't too keen: American Airlines and Caribbean Airlines said 'not in public'; El Al said 'not in the open'; and Pan Am said they preferred their mothers 'to be discreet'. It is perhaps best to tell the person at the check-in if you want to breastfeed and presumably they will allocate you a suitable seat.

Bottle Warming and Nappies

If you need your baby's bottle warmed most airlines, including charters, will do it for you. They should also be able to keep a bottle in the fridge for you (label it to avoid confusion) and supply boiling water for you to make up feeds. Try and keep the bottle with you for take off and landing, the sucking action will help stop your baby getting earache due to the change in pressure. Charter flights do not carry nappies but some scheduled airlines do. You may have to request them in advance (with British Airways, Pan Am and Alitalia for example). Some airlines that carry them on board routinely include: Canadian Pacific, SAS, Lufthansa (special babypacks with bibs, etc.), Swissair, British Caledonian (longhaul only), Austrian Airlines, El Al and Delta.

As for special nappy changing facilities, it rather depends on the plane. Some aircraft are fitted with fold down tables in toilets (Airbuses often have them), otherwise you have to make do on your lap. You will have to have patience and a lot of skill in manoeuvring in small places. Trying to change a baby in the aircraft loos is almost impossible. Personally I always do it on my lap and hang my neighbours.

Carrycots

'Mummy had to have the baby on her lap for 10 hours.'
(Sara, 7)

You may, at the discretion of the airline, be allowed to take your own carrycot on board a flight (even a charter flight). It is best to travel with a collapsible one just in case there isn't enough room and it has to be put in the hold. El Al are one of the few airlines that won't allow your carrycot on board. You will have to hold the baby for take-off and landing—yes, even if it does mean waking him up when he's just dropped off.

Scheduled Flights

Scheduled airlines vary considerably in what they provide for families. The facilities depend on the airline's policy towards children, the length of the flight and the size and design of the aircraft. Many facilities are only available on request and on longhaul flights. This means you have to ask for nappies, special meals or a skycot when you make your booking, rather than wait until you get to the airport.

Some airlines do a lot more for families than others. British Caledonian, for example, have 'Mothers Assistants' to provide help for any mother travelling with a young family. Although nappies, babyfood and milk are only available on longhaul flights, there is always a supply at the desk at the airport for emergencies. KLM have a wide range of babyfood on board, plus sleeping bags for older children, while SAS take a lot of trouble with their younger passengers, offering sleeping bags,

Disney mealboxes with games, cartoon films and cradles for babies as well as having nappies and babyfood on board. British Airways provide funpacks with activity books and games even on shorter flights, although nappies and babymilk are only available on request. Swissair's *Travel Tips for Families* says: 'diapers, babyfood and other useful accessories for the care of your little darling is standard equipment on all Swissair flights.' For more detailed information on who does what, see below. (The airline details are based on replies to questionnaires sent to over 70 airlines, of whom just over half replied. I have only included those that fly to holiday destinations.)

Skycots

Most scheduled airlines provide special cots for babies travelling on long distance flights (but some airlines, i.e. World Airways to the States, do not have them). These take various shapes and forms, some look a bit like the box you put your weekend groceries in and if your baby is big he may not fit in! Some airlines specifically tell you the maximum length your baby can be to fit into it (Canadian Pacific, for example, say 28 inches, Caribbean Airways 22 inches), so you will need to get out your tape measure! Skycots or whatever else they are called are usually fixed to the bulkhead; occasionally they hang from the luggage rack.

Special Menus, Babyfood and Milk

You will not get special meals on charter flights for children but a number of scheduled airlines will supply children's menus, jars of babyfood and milk on scheduled flights. Most require notice in advance. Ask when you book.

Books and Games

Again, you are unlikely to get anything for the children to do on a charter flight, although Monarch say they have games and books for children on request. On longer flights with scheduled airlines you may be offered a pack for the children (stick on games, activity books, crayons). If it doesn't arrive, ask for it. They should be available routinely with: World Airways, Canadian Pacific, Air Canada, American Airways, TWA, SAS, Swissair, Lufthansa, Pan Am, British Airways, Alitalia, Austrian Airways, British Caledonian, El Al and Delta.

Safety

You will usually not be able to sit with the children in the seats next to the emergency exits. Small children will have special life vests which will be given out by the stewardess as and when necessary. Unlike adults' vests you should inflate these before you leave the aircraft. You should try to keep your children's seat belts fastened (if you can) during the flight, particularly if they drop off to sleep.

Flying Clubs

If your child is a keen flyer he might like to join a flying club. Several airlines run them, including British Airways and British Caledonian. As well as membership cards and badges both airlines also have logbooks so your child can keep tabs of the number of miles he clocks up.

Unaccompanied Minors

If you want to send your child on a plane alone, British Airways (Young Flyers) and British Caledonian (Unaccompanied Minors) have special stewardesses who will look after them. Children (under 12) have their own check in desk and lounge at the airport and will be escorted to the plane. You may have to pay a fee if you want a personal escort for your child, although there are free hostesses on board for groups of children.

Special stewardesses escort children travelling alone.

Travelling by Car

'I like cars best because you can look out of the windows, on a plane everything rushes by.' (Mandy, 8)

Of all forms of transport, travelling by car is probably the most stressful with children in the back. Having to sit still in a cramped space for hours on end is not their idea of fun. Add to that a hot climate and the possibility of car sickness and a motoring holiday can turn into a distinctly unpleasant experience. However, whether or not you choose to spend the best part of your holiday behind the wheel or just use a car for getting there or touring around, the following tips should help to make it more enjoyable.

You basically have two choices when travelling with children: to put your foot down and get there as quickly as possible, ignoring the wails in the back, or to take it easy and stop frequently for loos and ice-lollies, perhaps giving up valuable holiday time. Only you know your family well enough to judge what's best for them and your sanity.

When to Do It

A touring holiday would not be top of my list for children from 6 months to around 4. Basically they are too young to get anything out of it, can't usually bear sitting still and will drive you potty by continuously asking when you're going to get there. Of course, there are exceptions. I just don't happen to know any. As a general rule try and keep in-the-car time down to a minimum with children of this age.

Touring with a very young baby isn't as bad an idea as you might think. Young babies are often rocked to sleep by travel and it rarely makes them sick. If the baby is in a carrycot you should have a restraint for it. If your baby is old enough to sit in a carseat and you are not taking your own car you can hire carseats, in this country and abroad, but don't expect him to sit in it if he's never had to before. It is also a good idea to have seatbelts in the back for older children. Over 5's don't seem to mind travelling in cars too much, so long as you supply things for them to do (anything from listening to cassette tapes to 'spotting' or quiz books, see p. 171). Older children are more likely to get carsick than younger children; if your child is prone to it, don't let him read and keep the air circulating (see health, p. 161).

'Luckily we had some travel sickness bags.' (Tom, 9)

Driving in the UK— Motorway and Roadside Service Stations

In a survey carried out by Trusthouse Forte's Little Chef restaurants, many holiday motorists said that the main reason they stopped at a roadside restaurant was to cope with restless children! As a result, Little Chef introduced special menus and facilities for babies and young children at over 250 Little Chefs and at around 70 Happy Eaters on main roads in Britain.

Although parents have become increasingly aware of the nutritional importance of food, it's unfortunately the old favourites that are offered up on the road. Over half the parents interviewed in Little Chef's survey said their children would be most likely to order chips as their first choice, followed by burgers, then sausages and fish fingers. Favourite 'afters' were ice-cream and Coke. As well as children's menus, Little Chefs have playgrounds, highchairs, and jars of babyfood, served in insulated feeding dishes with a sterilized spoon! Should you run out on the journey they also sell baby changing packs (including nappies, babywipes and a couple of plastic bags), and baby changing facilities are available in some Little Chef restaurants.

On motorways, Granada, Rank, RoadChef, and THF have children's menus in their restaurants, but if you want the children to be able to unwind, pull in at a Granada Service station. About half of them have imaginative outdoor play areas, where children can swing and scramble in and out of nursery rhyme equipment, like the 'shoe' of . . . there was an old woman who lived in a . . . You can also feed or change the baby in privacy. Most service stations have computer games, and shops.

Driving Abroad

'The English lights dazzle the French cars because they are on the wrong side so you have to have a thing on it so that it doesn't dazzle the French cars.' (Mark, 7)

Rules and regulations abroad are different from ours, particularly seatbelt laws and where children are allowed to sit in a car.

In Austria, Belgium, West Germany, the Netherlands, Norway, Switzerland and Yugoslavia children under 12 are not allowed to travel in the front seat. (In Austria and the Netherlands they can if they have a special child restraint.) In Yugoslavia even you aren't allowed to sit in the front as a passenger if you're 'visibly under the influence of alcohol'. In France, Greece and Luxembourg under 10's aren't allowed in the front, while in Denmark, Italy, Portugal, Spain and Sweden they discourage children of any age from travelling in the front (in Sweden they can if they have a child restraint).

Since traffic police are empowered to fine on the spot in many countries abroad it is worth sticking to the rules—even on a short ride down to the beach.

You shouldn't leave home without either the RAC's or AA's Continental Handbook.

Motorways

The motorway system throughout Europe is excellent, but you

Playgrounds at Granada service stations allow kids to let off steam.

have to pay tolls in some countries. If you do decide to use them, many northern European countries have efficient service areas with restaurants, shops, mother and baby rooms, special menus and playgrounds for children. Germany is particularly good (special signs denote what's available). Italy is pretty useless, and tolls are expensive.

Hiring a Car—and a Baby Seat

Wherever you go abroad you'll find a local carhire firm willing to part with a heap in exchange for a smaller sum of money than you would have paid for a better car with a reputable company. While it might not matter too much to you if you break down on your own, with a family in tow it is something you can do without. Don't risk it. Hire from a reputable firm. If you want a carseat fixed in the back you should book it in advance. You are unlikely to find a firm on the spot (lucky if you do, in Italy you stand a goodish chance). Either book direct through a carhire company (both Hertz and Avis have them) or your tour operator might be able to help (if you are going to Italy, Magic of Italy and Citalia will get you a babyseat in the back of a hire car).

Availability of babyseats with Hertz and Avis varies from country to country. Avis don't charge for them but Hertz do (from a nominal rental charge in Greece and Germany to almost £50 in Belgium). They also may only be available in the more expensive cars. For your interest: Hertz weren't able to offer me one in Malta, but could in France; Avis said they weren't normally available in France but they had them in Malta. Avis said that they could request one in Ireland, but if they didn't have one they would go out and buy me one—for free!

Wherever you go, request your baby's carseat well in

advance, particularly in the peak summer months. There's one other thing to consider if you are planning to hire a car abroad. If it is going to be very hot it is worth paying a bit more and getting a car with air-conditioning.

Seatbelts

More people are killed in motor accidents on holiday than by any other hazard. Make sure if you hire a car that it has seatbelts (in Italy lots of older cars still don't have them) and wear them!

Packing Up the Car

If you are taking the car it is always tempting to cram it too full. Before you start packing it up, take out the toolbox and stow it inside the car, so that if you break down you don't have to remove the entire bootful of luggage to get to it. Pack everything you'll need for the journey in the main body of the car, perhaps in a box or bag. One for food, one for changes of clothing (sickness and general accidents), one for toys and games. If you have a car cassette or your children have their own you can get a wide variety of tapes, suitable for all ages: nursery rhymes and fairytales for young children, quizzes, jokes and adventure stories for older ones, songs for all of you to join in on. You'll be surprised at just how much there is that is suitable for travelling. Good bookshops, like W.H. Smith, have a wide selection. A word of warning, do not take cassette tapes that come with books to follow. Not a good idea if you want to avoid the children being carsick. Whatever the ages of your children pack large plastic bags for rubbish, and plenty of drinks to keep them going if you don't want to stop continually.

Travelling by Ship

Ferries

'The car was strapped in to the Hovercraft because it might move round. When it started it felt like my tummy was left behind.' (Laura, 7)

Choosing which ferry to use if you are crossing the Channel or North Sea usually depends on where you are going to on the Continent, how quickly you want to get there and how much driving you want to do at the other end.

There are numerous different ferry companies, many operating on the same route. All ferry brochures are widely available in travel agencies. In general, children under 4 travel free, and under 14's get a reduction. Ages may vary slightly with each company. Some ships have playrooms and on board activities.

All-inclusive Holidays

Most of the shipping companies also offer all-inclusive holidays, where you take your own car (DFDS Longship, Hoverspeed

Continental Motoring Holidays, Brittany Ferries, North Sea Ferries, Sealink and Townsend among them). The best value with a family in the back are to get self-catering properties—a *gîte* in France, a holiday village in Holland, a log cabin in Sweden among them. They all also have touring holidays with special discount schemes at a number of hotel chains. Sometimes where two adults and two children are travelling together, the car goes free. Reductions for children are usually generous, particularly where under 15's or 16's are prepared to share your room. Ask your travel agent for current offers. The following ferry companies have good price structures and suitable family holidays.

'There's a restaurant on the boat and you can choose what you want to eat, you don't just have to eat what you get like on a plane.' (Henry, 5)

British Channel Island Ferries: Under 4's travel free. On all-inclusive holidays 4—13's are charged around half price if sharing hotel room with parents. Special family returns.

Brittany Ferries: Spain and France. Under 4's free. Good reductions on all-inclusive holidays, particularly to *gîtes* in France (over 750 to choose from), 4—13's pay a nominal flat fee. Playroom with toys for young children on board ships.

DFDS Seaways: Under 4's travel free. 4—16's get a berth at half the adult fare. If two adults and two children travel together, the car goes free. Generous reductions for children including free offers and nominal charges on all-inclusive packages. Under 16's or under 12's depending on route. Lots of self-catering holiday villages, farmhouses, chalets in Denmark, Sweden, Germany, Norway and Finland. Discos, cinema, saunas on board.

Fred Olsen: Sail to Norway and Denmark. Children's playroom on one of their ships. Under 4's free. 4—15's 50 per cent off.

Hoverspeed: Under 4's travel free. Reductions 4—14. Children free on all self-catering holidays and one child shares parents' room free at 2* Climat de France Fimotel, and first class Novotel and Mercure hotels.

Sealink: Under 4's travel free. Generous reductions for older children (vary between routes). Good offers on all-inclusive package tours. On sailings to Holland, for example, up to two children under 14 per adult travel free on day sailings with a car. Mother and baby facilities on all ships, limited range of nappies and creams. Supervised children's play areas on some ships. Competitions on board during the summer months. Commodore Club for young travellers under 15. £1 to join. At time of going to press, if children fill in the Stowaway Pass in the Sealink Car Ferry Guide brochure one month before you travel they are entitled to four free crossings—provided they take their family! The Club provides free magazines, posters, badges, etc.

Townsend Thoresen: Mother and baby facilities on most ships, Junior Sailor's Club (up to 14), entry forms in brochure, entitles members to logbook, various benefits, free entry to amusement parks abroad (if they take their parents). Under 4's travel free, 4–14's half price. All-inclusive packages (Motor Away, children under 14 go free on self-catering). Holiday villages with good family facilities in northern Europe.

Travelling by Train

UK

'I like the train better than the car because you can move around in a train.' (Jamie, 6)

Trying to change a baby in the loo of a British Rail train is probably worse than on a plane, although some newer Inter-City trains do have fold down tables in the loos. Try and attend to your children's toilet needs at the station. The major terminals have facilities for nursing mothers, and many stations have ladies' waiting rooms which have tables and chairs where you can breastfeed in comfort and relative privacy.

British Rail have a number of special deals for families and children. Basically, under 5's travel free, and 5's to 16's qualify for half fare. If children accompany a person with a Family Railcard (need not be a parent), over 5's and under 16's can travel for £1. Young Persons Railcards are also available for under 24's. Under 5's can eat free in restaurant cars; 5–11's at half price. You can put your bikes on the train, book ahead at stations.

Packages: Golden Rail Short Breaks cover London and other major cities as well as seasides, country-style breaks, and also rail/coach touring holidays of Wales and Scotland. Separate summer by the sea brochure, self-catering and hotels.

Abroad

Children under 4 travel free on trains in Germany, under 6's free in Austria, under 12's free in Denmark (provided you travel over 60 miles), under 16's free in Switzerland (with a special card, plus 50 per cent off for 16 to 25 year olds). Every country has its own rules and regulations! You can also nearly always get a family rail card entitling all of you to cut price travel. You usually have to buy them in this country before you set off. Ask a travel agent.

You can also buy a Rail Europ family card (from British Rail stations), valid for a year. It offers savings on rail and sea travel from Britain to 14 countries. It costs £5 and covers a minimum of three and up to eight people living at the same address. The holder pays the full fare while the others get the reductions. Discounts are up to 50 per cent abroad and up to 50 per cent on British Rail when you buy a through rail/sea ticket. You also get up to 30 per cent discount on the cross channel ferry.

Older children (under 26's) can buy one month's unlimited travel within 21 countries with an Inter Rail card. If you want to break your journey and explore you can often hire bikes at train stations, returning them further down the line. Both France and Denmark run a limited number of family trains with special facilities on board.

Packages: Golden Rail Great Little Escapes to the Continent by air and sea including hotels (mostly cities, also TGV trains through France, and the Glacier Express across Switzerland). Citalia (packages in Italy on Italian State Railways). French travel Service (France with SNCF). DER Travel (Germany with German Federal Railway). NSR Travel (Norway, Norwegian State Railways).

Motorail

'We put the car on the train and slept on it, you have to try and go to sleep by the noise of the train.' (Jack, 4)

If you're planning to drive long distances, perhaps to a holiday destination in France, Italy or Spain, you might consider putting your car on the train, at least one way. SNCF Motorail services run from Boulogne, Calais, Dieppe, Lille (45 miles from Dunkerque) and Paris to destinations throughout France, including Frejus/St Raphäel in the south, Milan and Madrid. Although it isn't cheap, you save on the cost of petrol, motorway tolls, hotels—and wear and tear on both you and your car!

While I haven't the space to cover train travel in every country in Europe, I think the situation in France is worth mentioning.

France

Children under 4 travel free on SNCF French Railways, 4–11's qualify for half fare. SNCF have special 'Family Trains' that operate on a number of routes throughout the summer. On these special trains 4–11's can get a *billet bambin* for a quarter of the adult fare (with their own seat or berth)—and have fun and games on board. Part of a carriage has been specially converted into a play area, with toys, monkey ropes, climbing frames, rocking horse and games to keep smallish children happy. There's also a separate area for warming bottles, a nursery for changing nappies, special children's menus for under 6's and 50 per cent reduction on meals for 6–12's.

A small number of 'Holiday Trains' operate during the summer on scenic routes throughout France. On board you'll find a French-speaking hostess who organises various competitions and games, artists or musicians. You may also get regional food specialities in the dining car.

If you want to break your journey you can stop off at intermediate stations and hire a car (reduced rates) or rent a bike through the Train + *velo* scheme that operates at 250 stations (bikes aren't suitable for under 7 or 8's), continuing the journey when you feel like it.

As in most countries you can buy a family ticket (Carte Famille): the first adult pays the full fare, any further adults 50 per cent and any child under 11, 25 per cent of the fare. SNCF have a booklet, *Votre enfant voyage en train* (in French), describing all the facilities for children on French trains.

Travel During Pregnancy

Many women carry on regardless during pregnancy, but if you are pregnant you should give travel a little extra thought. If you have to travel during your pregnancy the safest time to do so medically, provided everything is going normally, is from 18 to 24 weeks. The widely varying standards of medical care in different countries abroad is probably more important to take into account than the travel itself. If you are pregnant, you should think very carefully before going anywhere with poor medical facilities.

Medically it is not considered a good idea for any woman who has had previous miscarriages in later pregnancy to travel. If labour starts early, the safety of both you and your child will depend on the availability of expert medical care.

Travel in itself is not likely to cause a miscarriage but it can make you feel sick, particularly if you are in the first three months and you're already feeling queasy. There are some brands of travel sickness pills that are considered safe in pregnancy, although most cause some sort of side effects (drowsiness, dry mouth, blurred vision). Check with your doctor before you take anything.

Illnesses associated with travel (high fever through an infection or vaccination with a live virus or severe dehydration associated with diarrhoea) are much more likely to affect your pregnancy than the travel itself.

You should think carefully before embarking on long distance travel, and that includes places like The Gambia.

Inoculations

If you need a vaccination in order to travel to a foreign country you may get a reaction and a high fever with vaccines that use a live virus (yellow fever, polio). Diphtheria and typhoid vaccines can also produce a reaction and a high temperature. This is risky in pregnancy. Also a BCG jab (against tuberculosis) can affect the fetus. You should seriously consider avoiding travelling to places that need any of these jabs (which again includes places like the Gambia).

Malaria

While it is generally not advisable to take any pills during pregnancy, if you are travelling to a malarial zone it *is* important to take tablets to prevent infection. Several are accepted as being safe. Your doctor will advise you which ones to take, depending on *where* you are travelling to.

Air Travel

If your pregnancy is normal, flying in a pressurised cabin should have no ill effects. Airlines vary as to how pregnant they will let you be to fly with them. Some will let you make the return journey at 36 weeks, others won't take you if you are over 28 weeks. Iberia make no restrictions on pregnant women at all but on the other hand make their pregnant passengers sign a waive of liability before they'll carry them and require a medical certificate. Many airlines will take pregnant passengers up to 28 weeks without any special documentation. After that time most require a medical certificate which you can get from your doctor. Since the rules vary with different airlines, you will need to check beforehand. Do not leave it until you hand over your tickets; you may not be allowed to board the plane! Also check your holiday insurance to make sure pregnancy isn't excluded and that it covers you while you are away. Most policies do not cover the last two months of pregnancy (see insurance, p. 188).

If you have just had a baby or are pregnant you have an increased risk of developing a blood clot in your legs which can travel to your lungs and be fatal. Do not sit in a cramped position for too long, move your legs and wriggle your toes, get up and walk around at least once an hour. The same applies to sitting in a car—stop every hour or so and get out and stretch your legs.

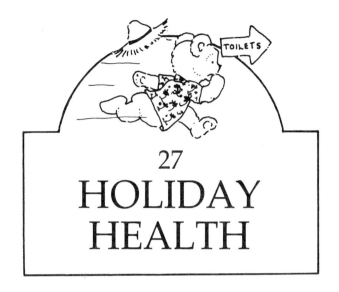

27

HOLIDAY HEALTH

For most parents, the most worrying aspect of going abroad is the thought of their children falling ill. Many holiday illnesses can be avoided if you pay special attention to cleanliness and obey some simple rules. The most common holiday complaint is diarrhoea—two-fifths of all international travellers suffer from it, 30 per cent of them badly enough to be confined to bed, and a further 40 per cent are so incapacitated that they are forced to change their itineraries. Hopefully you won't be one of them.

Diarrhoea

Diarrhoea still claims the lives of more children in the Third World than any other disease. As a holiday illness it is not usually severe, can be treated and, more importantly, can largely be avoided by following a few basic rules.

Prevention

Most travellers' diarrhoea is caused by micro-organisms that you get by swallowing contaminated food. They may be on your hands (so you should make sure the children wash their hands before meals) or the food itself may be contaminated. To avoid diarrhoea you and your family should stick to the following principles:

* Only eat 'hot' food that comes to the table steaming—send back anything that is warm and could have been lying around.
* Do not eat cold food, particularly meat, or ice-cream.

* Do not drink tap water; buy bottled water (check seals on bottles), fizzy is better than still. Give children well known brands of canned drinks rather than juices, milkshakes or squashes.
* Do not use ice in drinks, it is only as safe as the water it is made from. If in doubt, avoid it.
* Boil water to sterilise it for at least five minutes or use water purifying tablets (take them with you) for making up the baby's milk or packets, even for cleaning teeth in suspect places.
* Avoid locally made ice-cream (wrapped varieties are better) and yoghurts—it could have been made from unpasteurised milk (you may not get diarrhoea but could get brucellosis or tuberculosis).
* Avoid shellfish (they may have consumed bacteria from contaminated sea-water).
* Avoid unpeeled fruit, and salads—human faeces are sometimes used as fertilisers in the tropics. Bananas are safe and nutritious.
* Avoid rice, unless it is freshly cooked and comes to the table hot.
* Do not eat food that has had flies on it.
* Make sure children wash their hands regularly, certainly after going to the toilet and always before meals.
* Take along a stack of babywipes and use them frequently.

While most travellers' diarrhoea can be avoided by following these simple rules of hygiene, if you are travelling outside Europe diarrhoea can be a symptom of a more severe illness. Consult a doctor if symptoms persist, are accompanied by a high fever or if your child gets unduly sleepy.

Treatment

Children are just as likely to get diarrhoea as adults, but while adult bodies don't notice fluid loss so readily, diarrhoea in children can lead to severe dehydration. It was doctors in a refugee camp in Calcutta who demonstrated that dehydration and loss of body salts could be treated swiftly, cheaply and out of hospital by a simple remedy. What they came up with was described by *The Lancet* as 'potentially the greatest medical advance of this century'—the replacement of the body salts and sugars lost with loss of fluid. You can buy satchets of rehydration salts (like Dioralyte, Infalyte) from chemists before you go to make up when you get there or you can make your own with a special spoon you can get free from TALC (Teaching Aids at Low Cost). TALC was set up by Professor Morley of the Institute of Child Health to help children in the Third World. His solution to the problem was to let people make their own medicine, so he invented a two-ended plastic spoon for making home-made rehydration mixtures—one end for the salt, the other for the sugar, with the simple warning: 'taste—do not use if more salty than tears.' Available free (send sae) from TALC, PO Box 49, St Albans, Herts.

Whether you get yourself a scoop or buy a box of satchets, do not wait to use them. Most adults and children with mild diarrhoea improve so quickly after replacing the salts that the use of a constipating drug isn't usually necessary. You may want to control your diarrhoea if a bout happens while you are travelling and you are worried about finding loos. But while *you* might consider taking a remedy you should think carefully before you give anything, other than salts, to your children. Constipating drugs like diphenoxylate (Lomotil) and codeine phosphate act on the central nervous system as well as the gut and therefore should not be given to young children. There have been several cases of accidental poisoning with Lomotil in children under 5 and symptoms of overdosing can show with as little as one tablet. If you do decide to take a treatment to stop the symptoms, a locally acting drug like loperamide (available as Arret over the counter here, or Imodium on prescription) is probably the best one for adults and for children over 12, though you should follow dosages carefully. Do not give codeine phosphate to children under 9.

Antibiotics are usually not used in the treatment of diarrhoea; they are useless against almost all viruses and germs that cause diarrhoea. They may also cause diarrhoea themselves.

Travel Sickness

'If you feel sick in a car you should listen to the radio and look out of the window.' (Jenny, 4)

There is nothing guaranteed to ruin a journey more than the children throwing up all over the place. Some children get travel sick, others don't. If you know that yours do you can give them a tablet well before you travel to stop their being sick. Once the vomiting has started it is usually too late.

We get travel sick when we are travelling passively. You won't get travel sick on a bicycle or a horse but you may well on the back of a camel. The pilot, captain or driver won't get sick, but his passengers may. Those at the wheel can anticipate the ups and downs, swerves and bumps, the passengers can't.

Prevention

* Don't talk about it or ask children if they feel all right. It has been shown that the more you anticipate feeling sick the more likely you are to throw up.
* Give children things to do or listen to to take their minds off it.
* In cars, keep the windows open.
* Avoid eating greasy foods before travelling.

* Do not let children read in the car.
* Look ahead not out of the side windows.
* Older children should be allowed to sit in the front.
* Make frequent stops (hourly) and don't drive fast over hilly roads.

Treatment

Lots of brands of travel sickness pills make you feel sleepy and thirsty: Sturgeron is effective and it doesn't (at least in most people), and it has the added advantage of working for a long time. If children take it the night before you travel any slightly sleepy side-effects will have worn off, although you may, of course, want them to doze off, particularly on a long car journey. There are several other remedies available over the counter, like Kwells. You have to be careful to give the right dose. If your children are feeling slightly nauseous and you are in the car, stop and let them run around. Sips of Coke may also help stop the feeling of sickness as may keeping their head still and eyes shut. Once they've thrown up they will feel better. Pack some paper bags for emergencies.

Air Travel

Children and adults are less likely to get motion sickness when travelling by air. It affects only about one per cent of passengers (more if there is turbulence).

The most common problem travelling by air is earache due to the change of pressure; however, this is less likely in babies and young children. Coming down is more likely to cause earache than going up. The pressure can upset the middle ear and sinuses particularly if you have a cold or blocked sinuses.

Prevention

'Mummy always says to bring gum because when you land your ears hurt.' (Sally, 4)

To avoid discomfort you should give sniffly children a squirt of a nasal decongestant spray (like Sinex) or a few nose drops before you travel. No one with a heavy cold should travel by air as earache can be very painful. If your children tell you that they feel pressure in their ears, tell them to:

* Pinch their nose and with their mouth shut, blow out hard or swallow.
* Pinch their nose and drink.
* Move their lower jaw from side to side.
* Yawn or open their mouth wide.
* Suck sweets; or in the case of babies their thumbs, you or a bottle.

It is easy to get dehydrated on long flights. Encourage children to drink a lot and since their feet are likely to swell up, let them take their shoes off.

Jetlag

'When we got back to London it was teatime so we didn't have any lunch because we had breakfast on the aeroplane and we didn't have lunch because it was teatime when we got home.' (Mark, 6)

Children adjust faster to time change than we do. But an over-tired child does nobody a favour, not least of all on a long flight. If you really do want to regulate your child's sleeping patterns Phenergan can be useful for babies over 6 months but it has been shown to produce a sensitivity to light, so if you are going somewhere sunny your child's skin might come out in a rash. Check with your doctor before you go. When you get there you shouldn't be surprised if your children eat and sleep at odd times. Gradually bring them round to the new regime but don't try and force it. You won't be able to anyway. A few parents I know who travel to southern Europe keep their children on their own time, they go to bed later but sleep later in the morning too. If you are travelling longer distances, to the States, say, you will find that the children adjust more quickly than you do.

Hot Climates

Children adapt to a hot environment very quickly, especially thin, wiry, active children. Give them plenty to drink—enough to ensure that their urine is consistently pale in colour. Heat-stroke is caused by an acute loss of water and salt deficiency so you should replace salts lost in sweating, be liberal with it on food and give them plenty of drinks.

Sunburn and Heatstroke

Even the Mediterranean sun can be dangerously hot, especially at midday. Heatstroke can be dangerous in children, cause vomiting and a high temperate and severe dehydration. Keep up fluid intake by giving them lots of drinks.

Prevention

To avoid sunburn use a strong sunscreen, particularly at the beginning of the holiday. Uvistat is a good block although there are lots of other sunscreens than will totally block the harmful rays. Take exposure to the sun slowly. After an hour the first day, make children wear a T shirt and build up time in the sun gradually. Also:

* Never leave a baby in the sunshine; park the buggy or pram in the shade.
* Never leave a baby in a car, even with a window open.
* Make sure you don't overheat your baby, clothes should be cotton and kept to the minimum.
* Sunglasses and visors help protect children from the glare of the sun and avoid headaches.
* A hat will prevent sunburn on foreheads and faces and also help protect eyes.

Treatment

If your child's skin gets really sore, calamine soothes burnt areas and a painkiller (*not* aspirin) will relieve inflammation. Make them drink and allow the skin to heal before exposing it to the sun again. In severe cases you may need Indocin tablets or Indomethacin lotion to put on after exposure to strong sunlight.

Prickly Heat and Nappy Rash

Prickly heat can be very uncomfortable: the signs are tiny blisters on a slightly inflamed skin. It is usually caused by sweating. Your child may also get an irritation to seawater drying on the skin. Make children have frequent showers. Dry the skin gently, put calamine lotion and zinc oxide powder on and keep (cotton) clothes loose fitting. Don't keep the baby in a soggy nappy. If he gets nappy rash let air get to the skin and don't use plastic pants. Treat and help prevent, as you would do at home, with zinc and castor oil, or petroleum jelly.

Bites and Stings

Prevention

Take a good insect repellent with you like Autan (spray, stick or cream), or anything containing diethyl toluamide and keep applying it; some repellents are only effective for a few hours. Oil of Citronella seems to scare mosquitoes off (which is more than can be said for a little gadget that was on the market which produced a high pitched bleep. It has never been proven to work, and biting mosquitoes are apparently deaf!) If you are sitting down, mosquitoes go for the ankles first. Spray the repellent onto cotton socks and cover children up as soon as it begins to get dark or if you are walking in long grasses or near stagnant water.

Air-conditioned rooms should keep mosquitoes out but nets on windows have to be good ones to work. You can get impregnated strips (Z Stop) of Citronella to hang up in your room (or tent) or you can buy aerosol cans and spray the place, but the effects won't last the night. One of the most effective methods is the coil. You light one end and it burns slowly, giving off pyrethrum. Buy a good local brand. You can also buy a plug-in variety (Italian supermarkets have them)—a heating plate with a tablet in it that slowly vaporises. You have to have a nearby plug. Take a special net for the baby's cot and make sure mosquito nets on beds are hole free.

Treatment

The pain that arises after an insect bite is due to an allergic reaction. Each new bite makes all the others itch! Everyone reacts differently. Some people are more attractive to predatory insects than others. Try and persuade children not to scratch (keep nails short). Calamine lotion should stop the itching. Antihistamine tablets (Triludan will *not* make you sleepy) will also help, although antihistamine creams aren't such a good idea for hot sunny places, sensitivity can occur following exposure to light. If you know that you or your children react very badly to bites you could ask your doctor to prescribe a mild steroid cream (such as Betnovate) to use if the skin is not broken and there is no evidence of infection. If the skin does break and become infected you will need an antibiotic cream. Ask your doctor if you want to travel prepared.

Cuts and Grazes

Treatment

Clean the wound as soon as you can with an antiseptic lotion or cream or clean water. You should take with you a dry powder spray (like Savlon Dry) which does not sting, and plenty of plasters.

Creeping Eruption

Children on holiday spend a lot of time without their shoes on. If you are travelling to Thailand, Sri Lanka, West Africa, North America (Florida) or the Caribbean they can pick up hookworm larvae from dogs and cats by walking barefoot on beaches. The parasite is pretty harmless but wanders aimlessly under the skin, causing itching and sometimes blistering, particularly on the feet. See a doctor if you suspect it. Treatment is easy with Mintezol or skin can be cooled with ethyl chloride which also kills the larvae.

Immunisation

Most countries will let you in without specific vaccinations. But there are plenty that recommend certain immunisations and since it is an effective measure against some important diseases they are well worth having.

The DHSS free booklet, *Protect Your Health Abroad* SA 35

from DHSS Leaflets Unit (address below), contains a list of all the required and recommended precautions for all countries. More detailed information is contained in the WHO booklet: *Vaccination certificate requirements*. Or ask your doctor or a specialist centre (see opposite page). Requirements sometimes change so it is important to get up-to-date information.

You can get your jabs at specialist centres—you may have to make an appointment—or from your GP. Either way you'll have to pay. Some vaccines (like yellow fever) have to be stored at special temperatures so have to be given at designated centres. You may get a reaction, so leave plenty of time before you travel to get over it.

If you choose to discuss it with your doctor, do so at least a month before you intend to travel. Tell him where you are going, how you plan to get there, how old your children are, where you plan to stay and whether you have any stopovers. You may need several vaccinations, spaced over a few weeks with a booster before you go. Your children may be lucky, as they may well already be protected by the immunisations they have had routinely before starting school. They should have had inoculations against: diphtheria, whooping cough, tetanus, measles and polio. Most of them before they were 1 with a booster at 5. They will need another booster against tetanus and particularly polio if they are travelling to countries where these diseases are prevalent and they have not had one in the last five years.

Cholera and typhoid vaccines are not usually given to children under 1 year and yellow fever not below 9 months but young babies are much less likely to get these diseases, especially if appropriate precautions are taken. If you are breastfeeding, they will have your immunity. It is safe to give all other vaccinations to babies over 6 months.

Few vaccines provide 100 per cent protection so it is still very important to watch what you eat and drink. What they do is to stimulate the body's defence systems by injecting a small amount of the bacteria or virus concerned into the tissues. Some vaccines are 'live' and stimulate antibodies which are then ready to leap into action should a real infection happen. The number of injections you will need will depend on whether the vaccine is 'live' or 'killed' and whether or not you have had one before. If you've had an initial course against polio, tetanus and typhoid, all you'll need is a booster. The period of protection varies from six months (cholera) to ten years (yellow fever). You can also get an injection against hepatitis. It is usually given just before you go away and after all your other inoculations.

You no longer need smallpox immunisation. The disease has been completely eradicated due to the effectiveness of the vaccine. All of you should get a polio booster (which hasn't) if you haven't had one for five years, and/or you are travelling anywhere beyond Europe, except North America, Australia and

New Zealand. There is no injection involved, just drops of vaccine on a sugar lump.

Malaria

You can't be immunised against malaria but you can take tablets to prevent yourself from getting it. Babies from birth can get it and children should take anti-malarial tablets or syrups. The tablets differ according to the area you are travelling to (because of the different types of mosquito). If you are pregnant your resistance to malaria is low. The disease is more frequent and more severe and can affect the fetus. There is a very real danger of getting malaria in most of Africa, much of the Near and Middle East and most of South East Asia and Central and South America. It only takes one little mozzie to inflict the disease and he might be lurking on the aircraft gangway, even on a short transit stop. You have to take the tablets for a week before you travel and for a month after you get back. If you are travelling to a malarial area it is also worth trying to avoid getting bitten by taking a good insect repellent (see bites, p. 164), spraying your room or lighting one of those coils if you're camping. Try and put a net over the baby's cot. If possible, choose a hotel that has air-conditioning or nets over the windows. If there are mosquito nets over the beds check there are no holes in them. Take a sewing kit for instant repairs!

You do not have to worry unduly about travelling with young children to tropical countries, provided they have had the relevant vaccinations and you take proper precautions in the way of cleanliness and eating sensible foods. It is often more trivial complaints like cuts, bites, diarrhoea, coughs and colds that are more important once you're there.

Specialist Centres for Vaccinations/Advice

Check opening hours and whether you need an appointment.

British Airways Medical Service, 75 Regent Street, London W1. Tel: 01 439 9584.
Hospital for Tropical Diseases, 4 St Pancras Way, London NW1. Tel: 01 387 4411 (mornings only).
Bureau of Hygiene and Tropical Diseases, Keppel Street, London WC1. Tel: 01 631 4408.
PPP Medical Centre, 99 New Cavendish Street, London W1. Tel: 01 637 8941.
Thomas Cook Medical Centre, 45 Berkeley Street, London W1. Tel: 01 499 4000.

Government Agencies (leaflets, information)

DHSS Leaflets Unit, PO Box 21, Stanmore, Middlesex.
DHSS International Relations Division, Alexander Fleming House, Elephant & Castle, London SE1. Tel: 01 407 5522, ext 6749.

HMSO, PO Box 276, London SW8. Tel: 01 622 3316 (WHO booklet £4.20).

Scottish Home and Health Department, St Andrew's House, Edinburgh. Tel: 031 5568501, ext 2438.

Welsh Office, Cathays Park, Cardiff. Tel: 0222 825111, ext 3395.

DHSS, Dundonald House, Upper Newtownards Road, Belfast. Tel: 0232 63939, ext 2593.

Falling Ill Abroad—In Pregnancy

If you are pregnant and do get ill abroad, do not swallow pills randomly, particularly those you've bought over the counter for travel sickness or diarrhoea. Read the instructions on the packets carefully. You should check with your doctor at home which pills are safe to take should you need any. If you have to consult a doctor abroad be a little wary about it, especially in out of the way places where the doctor may not speak English. Awareness of the dangers of various drugs is not necessarily universally known. If you do not look pregnant and you have called in the doctor for a sore throat, tell him, he probably won't ask or guess if all he does is look down your throat! He may well prescribe something you should not be taking, like tetracycline antibiotics.

Drink plenty of fluids in hot places (avoids dehydration and the possibility of thrombosis). Eat bran or vegetables to avoid constipation, and don't eat undercooked meat as you could get toxoplasmosis. Although it only causes a mild illness in adults it can effect the fetus.

28
HOLIDAY
HEADACHES
& HAZARDS

Without sounding too alarmist there are a million and one things to watch out for when you are taking children away on holiday, especially abroad. The following are some questions you might like to have answers to before you book and some hazards to watch out for once you get there.

* If you are travelling with a baby or young child, try and find a holiday that comes with a: highchair, cot, indoor or outdoor playground, bottle warming facilities, early supper times, children's menus, shallow paddling pool, babysitters.
* Before you book your holiday find out how easy it is to get to the beach (trekking miles down and up cliffs or steps with all the equipment you need is to be avoided).
* Don't go anywhere that is too hot if you plan to spend all your time on the beach.
* Don't attempt anything other than the journey with a baby or toddler that involves hours at a stretch in the back of a car.
* If you plan to have a villa with your own pool try and get one with a pool that is fenced off.
* Check the safety of the cot before you put your toddler or baby in it (spaces between bars, sturdiness etc.).
* Check the safety of your balcony to make sure your child can't wriggle under it or get his head stuck.
* Check the depth of the shallow end of the swimming pool, and how quickly it gets deep.
* Never leave a young child swimming without supervision.
* Check safety of playgrounds (is equipment fairly new?).
* If you go to a holiday centre, holiday village or campsite try and make sure your chalet, villa or tent is as near to the main

complex as possible, so your child can nap or sleep while you are getting on with enjoying yourself.

* In a hotel, ask for a room on the first floor, near the restaurant. Many kids feel quite secure if they know you are just at the bottom of the stairs having dinner. But they don't if they are miles away down long corridors.
* Check sockets for safety and cover them if you have a toddler.
* On the beach don't let your child play in the sewage outlet, watch out for broken glass, ring pulls off cans, tar, etc.
* If young children are playing ball games watch them—if it goes in the sea they may not realise how far out they are swimming to get to it.
* Don't send a small child off to buy drinks or ices if you are on a crowded beach, unless you watch him all the time. You may be able to see him, but when he looks back he will not be able to see you with a mass of people in front of him.

29
HOLIDAY
BOOKS

Anything that can keep children amused, especially on the journey, is well worth taking on holiday. Books take up little room and a couple of good ones, particularly about where they're going and what they're seeing, could keep your children quiet for hours!

Here are a selection of holiday books I think are worth buying (or borrowing from the library), divided up into different subjects. I haven't included any joke, quiz, crossword, activity and puzzle books. It is well worth taking at least one with you.

Don't take too many books if you are off on a holiday where you are going to be spending most of the time out of doors. Don't take too few if you've got a long journey, or anticipate bad weather and having lots of time on your hands. Some of the books I have picked out are good if you run out of ideas for games, others help children to observe their environment and have an educational slant. All are fun and should be available from good bookshops.

Games

Usborne Book of Travel Games £1.75 (or separately, *Car Travel Games* and *Air Travel Games*). Games (everyone, except the driver, shut your eyes), puzzles, activities, facts both for on the journey and when you get there.
The Puffin Book of Car Games (Douglas St P. Barnard, Puffin, £1.25). Back Seat pastimes, 'spotting' games, and when you get there. Essential read for parents. Packed full of ideas for games you'd never have come up with yourself.

Famous 5 Adventure Games and *Asterix to the Rescue* (Hodder & Stoughton, £4.95). Thick paperbacks packed full of mysteries to solve, codes to crack and maps to follow. Comes in a wallet with dice, folding lunchbox and maps.

The Piccolo Book of Travelling Games (Deborah Manley & Peta Ree, Piccolo, £1.95). A grown up 'read' but packed full of ideas for all ages.

The Whizzkid's Whizzbook (Peter Eldin, Armada, £1.75). Funny little paperback of mad facts for kids travelling to *'anywhere from down the lane to up the pole'*. Includes quizzes, jokes, games to play on your own, how to read a holiday brochure (*bed linen changed every day—from room to room*), a real laugh for over 8's and parents alike.

Languages and Foreign Places

Junior Guides to . . . Spain, France, Britain (Usborne Pocket-books, 99p). Slim volumes packed with facts and information about different countries; includes separate sections on sights (things to spot in churches), architecture, vegetation, shops and food with clear illustrations. Plus separate guide/picture strip phrasebooks with language tapes for beginners. Suitable for 8 or 9 year olds and up. Also *Practise Your French* for 11 year olds upwards. Other titles: *Peoples of the World*, a colourful glimpse into the lives and homes of people around the world (customs, clothes, food and buildings). Suitable for 8−11's.

Globetrotters *Fun in . . . Italy, Spain, America, Greece, Germany, Switzerland, France* and *Britain* (Piccolo, £1.50). Enjoyable pictorial series for younger children. Each title has games, puzzles and activities, but with a difference, the clues are all 'foreign': dice game through Paris, join up the dots to identify Spanish dishes or Greek instruments, put the right head on the Queen's Corgi, etc. Well illustrated.

Wellington's Way to Learn . . . (Spanish, French). Large slim book with hardcover, packed with drawings of cartoon characters doing various things with speech 'bubbles' in two languages, plus quizzes and games. For older children. (Granada, £3.95)

My Passport to France (Fontana Lions, £1.50). Fun, jokes, and amazing facts. Over 8's.

The Cat in the Hat, Beginner Book Dictionary in French (£5.95). Large, bulky cartoon book of very easy phrases and words arranged alphabetically. Too big to take with you. But good 'starter' for before or after.

Seaside and Countryside

Usborne Spotter's Guides: excellent series, lots of titles, for example: *Animals, Tracks & Signs, Country Walks, Sea & Freshwater Birds, Seashore* and *Wild Flowers*. Lifelike illustrations, questions to answer, things to identify and colour in and a scorecard to see how much you've spotted. Slim volumes. £1.50. Larger, Usborne's NatureTrail Books on similar subjects, £2.25.

Observer's Series (Puffin, £2.95). Lots of titles: *Sea & Seashore, Old English Churches, Architecture, Bird's Eggs, Castles,* etc.

Althea Nature (Dinosaur) Series. For 3 year olds upwards. Lots of bright easy titles, for example: *Life in Ponds, Beside the Sea, Caterpillars to Butterflies.* £1.10.

Adventure and Sports

Getting About in the Great Outdoors (Anthony Greenbank, Puffin, £1.95). A book for older children, a definitive guide to outdoor activities, compiled by an Outward Bound instructor, practical advice (how to abseil, survive on a mountain, etc.). A good read for novices.

Maps and Things

Junior Atlas of Britain (AA, £4.95). Teaches children how to plan a route, understand scales, plus games and activities.

30
SHOPPING ABROAD

On the whole, unless you are going to Outer Mongolia or backpacking through the jungles of Africa, there is very little you can't get in most package holiday destinations if you are staying in a resort or near a town. You may not find exactly the same brand of whatever it is you're looking for, and it may well cost a bit more but you can rest assured that your baby will not run out of nappies or babyfood and, if your children insist on having them, you will almost certainly be able to buy a packet of cornflakes. Most European shops import quite a range of British products. However, if you know you are going to a remote spot, or are holidaying outside Europe, it is worth travelling with the basic needs of a young family. Wherever you go you should take with you a first-aid kit of medicines (see packing, p. 182).

Shopping for Babies

Nappies

'There are lots of babies here and yes, they all wear nappies.'
(Helpful postcard from mother of baby in Turkey)

All babies the world over wear nappies. But they don't all wear disposables. You can get them anywhere in Europe—but you may get a bit of a shock at the price. If you are going somewhere hot, let your baby go nappy free.

With the help of Thomas Cook, travelling mothers and National Tourist Boards, I've priced nappies in different holiday destinations. Shop around, the prices of different brands vary

Most children hate shopping, don't forget the buggy or a sling.

enormously, local makes will be cheaper than familiar ones. The cheapest places to buy are supermarkets and the bigger the box the cheaper they are. Pharmacies also stock nappies as do small grocers' shops in out of the way places. Look carefully at what you are buying, they may be pads rather than the Smarty Pant variety so you will need plastic knickers. Here's a rough idea of nappy costs in popular destinations abroad—based on a packet of 30 for a newborn baby, starting with the most expensive places:

Nappy Prices Abroad

Very expensive: Lanzarote, Minorca, Ibiza.

About twice as much as they are here: Majorca, Portugal, Italy, Tenerife, Gran Canaria.

A bit more than they are here: Austria, Corfu, Rhodes, Malta, Turkey.

About the same or cheaper than they are here: Costa del Sol, Crete, Denmark, France, Germany.

If you are going further afield, ask the Tourist Board or Embassy in this country beforehand about availability. Even if they do sell them, you will probably only find disposables in big cities. Also some Third World countries will only sell pads, so you will have to take plastic pants with you.

Do take enough nappies with you for the journey, even though some airlines (scheduled) have a few on the plane.

Babyfood

Babies everywhere in Europe and in the States are fed out of jars and packets in much the same way as they are here. Your baby will not go hungry. But if you are venturing further afield you should check on availability first with Embassies or Tourist Boards. The only problem is that you may not be able to get familiar brands and ranges. Even if you can they may be made to a different formula and will not necessarily taste the same. For example, Milupa, a German company, sell extensively in Europe. But the packets you will find abroad may not be familiar ones; not only do different governments have different rules about what goes into babyfoods and they adapt the foods accordingly, but foreign babies like different ranges. If you are looking for Milupa products you will be more likely to find them in pharmacies than in supermarkets. Although you will see a babyfood called Milupa in Spain, don't be surprised if your baby doesn't instantly take to it, the company has nothing to do with the Milupa we are familiar with.

The two other familiar brands you might find abroad are Beechnut and Heinz.

If you are trying out locally made jars you can always ask a pharmacist to recommend a brand. The consistency of local brands may not be the same as our jars. If your baby is only used to strained food some of the jars available abroad may have too many lumps in them for his liking.

Check contents for additives: some countries are stricter than others about what they feed their babies. Watch for added sugar and salt. Also check on whether cereals are added to products, you may not want to feed a young baby with wheat. You can also get gluten free products in some countries (certainly Italy).

Do not expect your baby enthusiastically to consume every jar you put in front of him. Buy a few varieties and let him sample them until he finds the ones he likes. Better still, especially if you are self-catering, forget about jars and feed your baby (if he's over 5 or 6 months) on a diet of fresh fruit (mashed up), cheese, eggs and yoghurt with a bit of local honey.

The following is a list of which countries import familar brands of babyfoods. Do not assume that every shop will sell them— your best bet is to look for a large pharmacy or supermarket in a main town or city.

Beechnut are sold in Malta, Greece (but not smaller islands or Crete), Cyprus, Tenerife and Menorca.

Heinz sell their babyfood in Belgium, France, Germany, Gibraltar and Malta, though they may be manufactured in Canada or Holland. They also sell in Italy under the Plasmon label; a large variety (including tiny pasta shapes) are very widely available.

Milupa sell weaning foods in Germany, Belgium, France, Greece, Italy, Holland, Austria, Portugal, Cyprus, Denmark, Hong Kong, Yugoslavia, Malta, Kuwait and Oman. Not Spain, Israel, Africa or the States.

You can usually get some sort of rusks and biscuits. Farleys sell in Malta.

Take supplies of babyfood with you if you are going to North Africa, Crete, Israel, or anywhere further afield.

As well as these familiar brands you may also see Gerber and Nestlé products abroad but your baby will probably never have tasted them as neither sell in this country. One of the problems with introducing a baby to new products while you are away is that he may get addicted to them and then start rejecting his old foods when he gets home. Nestlé, who have an office here but don't sell in Britain, constantly get asked by mothers where they can get foods their babies have decided they like while they were on holiday abroad. Unfortunately they have to tell them they just aren't available over here.

Babymilk

Any baby will tell you that the formula he's used to is best and that anything else tastes awful. You will be able to buy powdered babymilk to make up into feeds almost everywhere abroad but brands may not be familiar and even if they are the formulas will not necessarily be the same. It is far better to take your own. If you run out take the empty tin or packet to the local pharmacy to find the nearest, similar brand. If you are buying locally you should make absolutely sure you are buying milk formulated for a baby not just dried milk which will be unsuitable. Milupa sell baby formula in the countries that they sell babyfood in (see above), except for Denmark, Hong Kong and Yugoslavia. They also sell a limited amount in the States.

Work out how much milk you will need and take tins (unopened) with you, to make up when you are there. I say *unopened* because I once packed an opened tin (in a plastic bag with a tie on it) in my suitcase. It exploded in flight and covered everything in my case in a white film of powdered milk. I had to wash the lot when I got there and do battle with the local ants for the entire holiday.

Never make up milk in advance and keep it warm in a thermos, it will be a breeding ground for bacteria. Put boiling water in the thermos and make up bottles as and when you need them. Use boiled water, mineral water from bottles or water to which you've added water purifying tablets to make up feeds.

If it is essential for you to find out whether you can get babyfoods in specific countries (for long trips for example), you can contact the manufacturers in advance and they should be able to tell you if you can expect to get their products.
Milupa (Tel: 0895 59851); Heinz (01 573 7757); Nestlé (01 686 3333).

Food Shopping

See the chapter on self-catering for the results of the Thomas Cook shopping basket survey of the cost of buying food abroad (p. 96). In general, butter, tea and beer can be very expensive abroad, so can coffee. It is well worth taking your own tea and coffee if you are renting a villa or apartment. When you are shopping in local supermarkets you may see a lot of familiar brands of food in holiday destinations, but local brands will always be cheaper. If your children can't survive without cornflakes or the like most larger resorts in France, Italy and Spain will stock familiar brands (though they will be much more expensive than they are here). You will be less likely to find familiar cereals on a Greek island and even I admit to taking Weetabix abroad with me when Emily was a toddler.

Do try local foods on your children. Local cheeses are far more interesting and nutritious than processed slices for example (try giving your baby a piece of Parmesan cheese to gnaw on if he's teething). You almost certainly won't be able to get squashes for the children (either to dilute yourself or in bars), but you will usually be able to buy sugar free juices and bottled water. You can't, for example, get rose-hip syrup or Ribena in Italy (though the Italians aren't averse to colouring water with wine for their children).

Medicines and Toiletries

Medicines can be difficult to get if your grasp of the foreign language isn't very good. The local pharmacist may be very helpful if you try and explain what the problem is. Try and avoid buying local products which contain a bit of everything in the hope that one of the ingredients will treat whatever you have. It is far better to take with you remedies that you might need. Sunscreens are always available abroad but can be a lot more expensive. Buy medicines from a pharmacist and toiletries from a supermarket.

Film

Film abroad is almost always more expensive than it is here, especially if you attempt to buy it in tourist resorts or near to sites of interest. Also the film may well be out of date and have been lying around in the sun. Obviously towns and bigger places have photographic shops but you will not necessarily be near to one when you run out of film. If your child has a camera that takes a cassette film, buy it here as you may not be able to get it abroad. Film is usually cheaper at the duty-free shop at the airport (although you can't always get black and white and sometimes only transparencies not colour print film). It is very expensive indeed in Majorca and Ibiza.

31

PACKING

Children may be small but they need an awful lot of paraphernalia on holiday. Clothing is the least of your worries, it's the umpteen teddy bears, reading books, cricket bats, cassette tapes, buckets, spades and tennis rackets that take up all the space. Add to that the baby's potty, feeding dish, nappies, bottles and the buggy and you may begin to feel you've made a big mistake.

If you haven't taken your child away before you may find you need a fair amount of equipment. If you can, borrow from friends. If not, Mothercare sell everything you need from travel cots and travel bags to portable highchairs and chair harnesses. It is also worth getting the catalogues of the Heinz Baby Club and Kiddy Mail (both mail order). The Kiddy Mail has a few additional items like an inflatable potty and an inflatable bath! (For addresses see back of book.)

Think logically, make a big pile of what you think you need, then reduce it by half. If you are going anywhere hot you will need far fewer clothes and if you take cottons they can be washed through and will dry within hours. There is really no need for young children to have anything more than three T shirts, two swimming costumes, one sweatshirt, one pair of long trousers, two pairs of shorts, underpants, socks, trainers and sandshoes. Let them travel in their tracksuits.

As for games and toys, cut them right down. I've often let Emily travel with six paperbacks she insists she'll read, activity books, travel draughts, pens and notebooks. Apart from on a plane or train she hardly touches them. Depending on the age of your child, one fattish activity book and a couple of pentel pens, a good paperback, toy car, doll or Rubik cube will do for short periods of boredom. A ball or a skipping rope is a good idea for when you get there, but unless your children are avid sportsmen forget about the tennis rackets, you can always buy a cheap local game there. Wherever you take your children it will be a new environment and most kids will be quite happy running around and exploring. If you are going anywhere like a holiday camp or activity centre you'll only need things for the journey.

The Journey

Always reckon for delays. All children over the age of 2 should be given their own rucksack (well labelled) into which you pack: the favourite toy or blanket that they can't sleep without, a drink and snack, a couple of pens, a notebook or activity book, a book to read, and a small toy to talk to. You can buy miniature travel games in which the pieces are kept on by magnets. But I've yet to meet a child who will sit still for long enough at an airport or on a ferry to play a game, although it might be an idea to invest in one if you have two children of similar ages in the back of the car. Avoid taking anything that comes in pieces, you're bound to lose some of them. It's usually much more fun for children to buy something in an airport shop or at a motorway service area. You can get toys, comics, travel games, cassettes for the car radio and books.

Packing Bags Checklist

This is a checklist for you and your children. It is not a list of all the things you should be taking with you. What you take will depend on the age of your child, what you plan to do and the climate. You'll need far less if you are going to a hot place than if you are going skiing or somewhere in Britain!

Activity books (puzzles, drawing, jokes)
Anoraks
Babygrows (cotton)
Babywipes
Ball
Beaker
Bib
Books
Bowls and spoon
Buggy (preferably lie-back)
Camera
Carrycot
Cassettes (for the car or tape recorder)
Contraceptives
Cotton socks, pants
Crayons
Credit cards
Disposable nappies (small number for travelling)
Drinks (bottle, thermos, or cartons for the journey)
Eurocheques
Favourite toy, cuddly, doll, bear (hand luggage)
Film (expensive abroad)
Food (for the journey, jars and packets)
Fly net, cat net (for carrycot)

Macs (plastic)
Mat (plastic to lie on)
Nightwear
Notebook (drawing)
Packets/jars of food for the
    journey
Passports
Pens (pencils, crayons,
    pentels)
Pills (any you or your children
    take regularly)
Plastic bags
Plastic mac
Plastic mat
Plastic sheets (cots, small kids'
    beds)
Playing cards
Purse (pocket money)
Potty, inflatable or ordinary
Rucksack
Shawl (lightweight for
    covering baby in buggy)
Shirts (long and short
    sleeved)
Shoes (canvas for sand,
    plastic for pebbles,
sandals or flip flops)
Shorts
Sling
Snacks (raisins, nuts, fruit,
    crisps)
Straps (for highchair, cot,
    toddling)
Sunblock/screen
Sunglasses
Sunhat
Sun umbrella (large and clip-
    on for the buggy)
Swimwear
T shirts
Thermos flask
Tickets
Trainers
Travel cot
Travel highchair
Travel wash (Dylon do a cream
    in a tube)
Trousers (or jeans, long cotton
    for cover ups)
Visa (USA)
Visor
Wellies

Packing for Self-catering

In addition to linen, towels, clothes, games and toiletries:

Candles (power cuts)
Clingfilm
Corkscrew
J cloths
Knife (one sharp one)
Matches
Mouli (food grinder)
Penknife (picnics)
Plastic bags (storing food)
Silverfoil
Small change (meters,
    phones)
Soap
String
Teatowels
Tin opener
Toilet paper
Torch
Small screwtop plastic
    containers containing
    quantities of: salt, pepper,
    washing up liquid, oil,
    sugar, teabags, coffee
    and squash—to avoid
    buying large bottles
    or packets when you get
    there and only using half
    of them.

Medical and First Aid Kit

You can buy travel kits at Boots and Mothercare or make up your own. I've given a number of drugs you can buy over the counter but read packets carefully or check with your doctor about different dosages for different ages of children.

Aftersun (soothes sunburn)

Painkillers (soluble or liquid paracetamol for younger children)

Calamine lotion (sunburn, bites)

For diarrhoea (Arret (over 12's) or kaoline mixture; rehydration sachets, like Dioralyte, for replacing salts)

Travel sickness pills (Stugeron)

Antiseptic (Savlon Dry antiseptic powder, spray on for cuts and grazes)

Oil of Eucalyptus (removing tar)

Oil of Citronella (deterring mosquitoes)

Insect repellent (containing diethyl-toluamide)

Petroleum jelly

Plasters

Zinc and castor oil cream (nappy rash)

Vaseline (sore bottoms)

Water purification tablets (Boots or Potable aqua)

Anti-malarial tablets or syrup (where necessary)

32
PASSPORTS
& HOLIDAY
INSURANCE

Passports

Any new addition to your family should be added to your passport automatically to save a panic when you decide to travel abroad. Children of any age can have their own passports but most parents get them added to their own. You should allow at least six weeks for a postal application to the Passport Office at Petty France in London during the peak summer months. And at least one month if you are applying in the provinces.

You can call in person but you will have to be prepared to wait. Children have to have their own passports as soon as they reach their sixteenth birthday. Application forms are available from travel agents, main post offices or your nearest regional Passport Office.

London Passport Office, Clive House, 70 Petty France, London SW1H 9HD. Tel: 01 213 3434.

Liverpool Passport Office, 5th Floor, India Buildings, Water Street, Liverpool L2 0QZ. Tel: 051 237 3010.

Newport Passport Office, Olympia House, Upper Dock Street, Newport, Gwent NPT 1XA. Tel: 0633 56292.

Peterborough Passport Office, 55 Westfield Road, Peterborough Cambs. PE3 6GT. Tel: 0733 895555.

Glasgow Passport Office, 1st Floor, Empire House, 131 West Nile Street, Glasgow G1 2RY. Tel: 041 332 0271.

Belfast Passport Office, Hampton House, 47–53 High Street, Belfast BT1 2AS. Tel: 0232 232371.

Office hours: Monday to Friday, 9am to 4.30pm.

British Visitor's Passports

If you have to go away in a hurry and you've forgotten to add your child to your passport you can get a British Visitor's Passport immediately from the Post Office (Monday to Friday). They are about half the cost of a normal passport. They are only valid for a year, for holidays of up to three months, and to certain countries in Western Europe (not Scandinavia or the USA). You can get them for children up to 16. Under 8's can't have their own and have to be included on their parent's, step-parent's, adoptive parent's or brother's or sister's British Visitor's Passport (but not grandparents). If under 8's are travelling alone they must have their own proper passport.

Teddy Bears

International Bear Passports are issued by the United Kingdom of Teddy Bears and are available from the International Teddy Bear Club whose headquarters are in the Trocadero Centre, Piccadilly, London W1. Tel: 01 437 6706. Passports look very like the real thing, except that they are brown not blue. Teddy bears should apply with passport sized photograph either in person or by post. They have to fill in a form with details of their height,

Some teddy bears have all the luck!

occupation and place and date of birth, plus disclose any distinguishing features (chewed ear, one eye, etc.). Allow at least 28 days for postal applications to be dealt with (price: £5).

Immigration officers when presented with a teddy bear's passport will stamp it, provided bear and picture match. So far no bears have been refused entry into any country (they are exempt from visas for the States). However, the Home Office warns bear owners that 'immigration officers who refuse to stamp a teddy bear's passport would not necessarily be doing it out of spite, but because they regard the stamp as part of their authority and would not want it misused'. Teddy bears planning to abuse the system should think again—going on holiday is no picnic!

Holiday Insurance

'We didn't take out insurity (sic) and a car went into the back of us, Daddy was very angry.' (Nicki, 8, USA)

Although it is essential to take out holiday insurance for yourself (and the car) if you are travelling abroad a lot of people forget about the children, or think vaguely that if something happens to them they will be covered on their policy. This is not so. It is very important to take out a policy for each child travelling with you (although under 2's are sometimes included in their mother's policy).

The main things you are insuring against are cancellation or curtailment of your holiday; medical expenses; loss of, or damage to, baggage, money and valuables; personal liability; and accidents causing death or disability. Some policies also cover you or your children (should you fall ill) being flown home in an emergency. Not a very jolly thought, but one that is essential to think about before any trip you take abroad.

Most policies have a limit under each section as to how much you can claim. For example, up to £50,000 if you fall ill and have to pay for medical treatment. Some are unlimited. Make sure you take out an adequate amount and err on the generous side. The limit is usually higher for the States where the cost of medical treatment is exhorbitant.

With most policies there will be an excess, which stops you claiming for small amounts. This means that you will not be covered for the first £10 or £15 say. You should read the small print carefully, particularly to see what the policy excludes— sometimes pregnancy and often 'dangerous' sports like water-skiing, yachting and power-boating.

All members of your holiday party will be charged separately, but don't assume that because you've given one name all of you will be included. If you are buying a package tour, the tour operator will usually offer you the option of his own insurance, but few tour operators offer any reduction for children travelling with you. You do not have to buy this but can shop around until you find a policy that suits you. Premiums and cover vary considerably from company to company. Although you can get insurance at a family rate and sometimes reductions for children, check carefully how much cover children get and compare the costs with other companies. You may find you are paying more as an adult to qualify for the discount for your child. Also check your own broker; your household policy may cover you for some aspects of travel, so you may be duplicating cover if you take out a comprehensive travel insurance.

Medical Insurance

Insurance to cover medical eventualities will be included in your general holiday insurance policy. The amount should be enough to cover the cost of medical treatment and expenses incurred as a result of illness or injury (up to £50,000 is usually considered adequate). Most policies will also cover any travelling or accommodation expenses you may need as a result of your illness. Some will also fly you and your family home in an emergency. Choose a policy that offers a 24hr emergency service. You will be given a telephone number to ring should you or your family fall ill. In theory this should mean that the insurance company will speak to the doctor or hospital direct and reassure them that bills will be paid. They should also arrange for you or your family to be brought back to the UK for treatment, using, if necessary, special air ambulances with trained staff on board. Where possible, however, they buy seats on a scheduled flight—and perhaps send a doctor or nurse to travel with you. As with all policies these 24hr emergency services have their exclusions too. So read conditions carefully.

With policies that don't offer an emergency service, medical costs are usually only paid out when you get home and after you have filled in the form. It may therefore be necessary for you to part with large sums of money on the spot. Not all doctors and hospitals abroad will accept your insurance documents as evidence that they will eventually get paid, although if you or your family are in need of long-term treatment it is often possible for the insurance company to make arrangements to pay the costs directly.

Form E111

If you are travelling to an EC country, Eastern Bloc countries and most other West European countries you are entitled to free or reduced cost medical treatment. The method of claiming depends on where you are and, in the EC, whether you have the correct forms with you. In non EC countries you may be able to produce your passport. Wherever you go it is worth taking the families NHS medical cards and your driving licence with you.

To claim medical costs in EC countries you will need to

produce a Form E111 which you have to get before you travel. Leave as much time as possible before you set off to get hold of it, at least six weeks if you can. To get it you have to fill in leaflet number SA 30, called Medical Costs Abroad. You can get this at your local social security office or by dialling 100 and asking for Freephone DHSS or write to Leaflet SA 30, 'Medical Costs Abroad', DHSS Leaflet Unit, Stanmore, Middlesex. When you get it you will have to fill in the form CM1 which is inside the leaflet and then take it back to the DHSS. Keep your Form E111 inside your passport. SA 30 also lists other countries where you are entitled to free or reduced cost treatment.

Although Form E111 entitles you to a refund of your medical expenses, getting the money is sometimes difficult and involves more form filling. Sometimes you will have to pay the doctor on the spot and then reclaim. Keep all your receipts.

Falling ill or having an accident abroad can be very expensive as well as distressing—make sure you are properly covered.

Good Deals for Families

Credit Cards: If you are paying for your holiday by credit card either through your bank or your charge card you may get automatic travel accident insurance for you and your family, but cover varies. You may also get free medical insurance. Diners Club, for example, will extend their accident and medical cover to the whole family (including mother-in-law), where tickets and/or half of the expenses are charged to their card.

Tour Operators: Most of the major tour operators will insure under 2's travel free but older children pay the full amount. Wings (OSL, Sunlight) give a small discount for children from 2–16.

Insurance Companies: Europ Assistance have special family rates if you are travelling with children under 16. Also if your state of health leaves the children without anyone to look after them while you are away they will pay for them to get home under expert supervision. They have a well established 24hr emergency repatriation scheme. (Tel: 01 680 1234.)

ABC Apple Booking Company offer half price premiums for children under 16 and free insurance for infants, plus a 24hr emergency service. (Tel: 04023 49388.) If you are a member of a private health scheme you may get special rates; BUPA, for example, offer your first child (under 18) medical cover for less than half price and free medical cover to all other children.

Exclusions

Some policies exclude pre-existing conditions and dangerous sports.

Pregnancy may be excluded altogether, or you may only be covered with a doctor's certificate. Read your policy carefully, most policies *will not cover you for the last two months of pregnancy*, although Europ Assistance extend their cover to 38 weeks (if the baby is born prematurely it will not be covered).

Dangerous Sports: You may have to pay an extra premium for sporting activities like skiing, but again read small print carefully to see if any other sports you might be contemplating (like riding a motorbike, or watersports) are excluded.

33
REFERENCE BOOKS

Activity & Hobby Holidays (English Tourist Board)

Adventure and Special Interest Holidays in Scotland (Scottish Tourist Board)

Camping and Caravanning in Europe (AA)

Children's London (LVCB), from Tourist Information Centres or from Sales Dept., LVCB, 26 Grosvenor Gardens, London SW1 W0DU

England's Seaside (English Tourist Board)

Family Favourites—Your Holiday Choice (Robin Dewhurst, Gillian Thomas, Corgi)

The Family Welcome Guide (Jill Foster, Malcolm Hammer, Sphere)

Farm Holidays. A Guide to Farm & Country Holidays (Farm Holiday Bureau in association with the English Tourist Board)

Good Holiday Cottage Guide (Swallow Press, PO Box 21, Hertford SG14 2BH. £2.50)

Good Overseas Villa and Cottage Guide (Swallow Press, PO Box 21, Hertford SG14 2BH. £2.50)

The Good Skiing Guide (Consumers' Association and Hodder & Stoughton)

Guesthouses, Farmhouses and Inns in Britain (AA)

Guesthouses, Farmhouses and Inns in Europe (AA)

Holiday Homes, Cottages and Apartments in Britain (AA)

Holiday Which? (Consumers' Association, on subscription from 14 Buckingham Street, London WC2)

Kids' Britain (Betty Jerman, Pan). Everything for kids to do and see in Britain

Kids' London (Elizabeth Holt and Molly Perham, Pan)

Let's Go. Short breaks in England (English Tourist Board)
The Peaudouce Guide (29 Priory Street, Ware, Herts.)
Self Catering in . . . France, Italy, Spain, Portugal and *Greece* (Christopher Helm) 5 titles
Travellers' Health (Richard Dawood, Oxford University Press)
Where to Stay Guides: lots of titles, published by ETB and BTA. Also separate Where to Stay Guides for Wales and Scotland: *Self Catering Holiday Homes and Holiday Centres*. Also *Hotels, Guesthouses and Universities*; *Farmhouses, Bed and Breakfast Inns and Hostels*; *Where to Stay — Camping and Caravan Parks, Britain* (BTA)
Working Holidays UK and Abroad (The Central Bureau)

Books published by the English Tourist Board or British Tourist Authority are available from bookshops or from Tourist Information Centres.

34
BOOKING ADDRESSES & TOURIST OFFICES

Holiday Contacts

(Tour operators, travel companies, mail order, clubs and organisations.) Brochures from tour operators and travel companies not listed below can be found in most travel agencies.

American Round-Up, 315 Oxford Street, London W1R 2BQ. Tel: 01 499 3922.

Anglo-Dutch Sports Ltd, 30a Foxgrove Road, Beckenham, Kent. Tel: 01 650 2347.

Automobile Association, Fanum House, Basingstoke, Hants. Tel: 0256 20123.

Best Western Hotels, Vine House, 143 London Road, Kingston upon Thames, Surrey. Tel: 01 541 0033.

Blakes Holidays, Wroxham, Norwich, Norfolk. Tel: 0533 701701.

British Waterways Leisure, Hire Cruiser Office, Nantwich Basin, Chester Road, Nantwich, Cheshire. Tel: 0270 625122.

Brittany Ferries, Millbay Docks, Plymouth PL1 3EW. Tel: 0752 221321.

Butlin's Holidays, Bognor Regis, West Sussex PO21 1JJ. Tel: 0243 820202.

Cabin Holidays (*see* Canvas Holidays).

Camp Beaumont, West Street, Godmanchester, Cambridgeshire. Tel: 0480 56123.

Camping and Caravanning Club, 11 Lower Grosvenor Place, London SW1. Tel: 01 828 1354.

Canberra Cruises, 77 New Oxford Street, London WC1. Tel: 01 831 1234.

Canvas Holidays, Bull Plain, Hertford, Herts. Tel: 0992 59933.

Caravan Club, East Grinstead House, East Grinstead, West Sussex. Tel: 0342 269 44.

Center Parcs, Chapel Bar House, Maid Marian Way, Nottingham. Tel: 0602 414141.

Cerbid Quality Cottages, Cerbid, Solva, Haverfordwest, Pembrokeshire, Wales. Tel: 03483 573.

Châteaux en France, Bignor, Nr. Pulborough, West Sussex. Tel: 07987 366.

Citalia, Marco Polo House, 3–5 Lansdowne Road, Croydon CR9 1LL. Tel: 01 686 0677.

Club Méditerranée, 106–108 Brompton Road, London SW3. Tel: 01 581 1161.

Club Robinson, Olympic Holidays, 17 Old Court Place, Kensington High Street, London W8. Tel: 01 229 2411.

Club Valtur, Serena Holidays, 40/42 Kenway Road, London SW5. Tel: 01 244 8422.

Consumers' Association, 14 Buckingham Street, London WC2 6DS. Tel: 01 839 1222.

Colony Holidays, Grosvenor Hall, Bolnore Road, Haywards Heath, West Sussex. Tel: 0444 458621.

Consort Hotels, Tyedale Building, Piccadilly, York. Tel: 0904 643151.

Courage Pub Holidays (sae to Ted Ellway), Tavern An Carow, Station Road, Liskeard, Cornwall.

Crest Hotels, Bridge Street, Banbury, Oxon. Tel: 0295 67722.

Crystal Holidays, Alexandra House, 130–140 Alexandra Road, Wimbledon, London SW19. Tel: 01 879 0555.

Days Inn (USA), 15A Turk Street, Alton, Hants. Tel: 0420 87144.

DER Travel Service, 18 Conduit Street, London W1. Tel: 01 486 4593.

DFDS Longship Holidays, DFDS Seaways, Parkeston Quay, Harwich, Essex. Tel: 0255 554681.

Dolphin Adventure Holidays, 34–36 South Street, Lancing, West Sussex. Tel: 0903 765581.

Embassy Hotels, 34 Queen's Gate, London SW7. Tel: 01 581 3466.

England Holidays, Dept. D., ETB, Bromells Road, Clapham, London SW4.

English Country Cottages, Claypit Lane, Fakenham, Norfolk. Tel: 0328 51155.

Eurocamp Travel Ltd, Edmundson House, Tatton Street, Knutsford, Cheshire. Tel: 0565 3844.

Falcon Family Holidays, 33 Notting Hill Gate, London W11. Tel: 01 221 6298.

Forestry Commission, Public Information Div., 231 Corstorphine Road, Edinburgh. Tel: 031 334 0303.

Fred Olsen Lines, 11 Conduit Street, London W1. Tel: 01 409 3275.

Freedom Holidays, 224 King Street, London W6 0RA. Tel: 01 741 4686.

Gîtes de France, 178 Piccadilly, London W1. Tel: 01 491 0914.

Golden Rail, PO Box 12, York. Tel: 0904 642751.

Haven Leisure, Swan Court, Water House Street, Hemel Hempstead HP1 1DS. Tel: 0442 233111.

HCI, 4 Broadway, Fiveways, Edgbaston, Birmingham B15 1BB. Tel: 021 643 2727.

Heinz Baby Club, Vinces Road, Diss, Norfolk. Tel: 0379 51981.

Helpful Holiday Agency, Coombe Farmhouse, Chagford, Devon. Tel: 06473 3593.

HF Holidays, 142–144 Great North Way, London NW4. Tel: 01 203 0433.

Highlife Breaks (Thistle Hotels), PO Box IRA, Newcastle upon Tyne. Tel: 0632 321073 or 01 889 9336.

Hobby & Leisure Holidays, Bridge Street, Banbury, Oxon. Tel: 0295 67722.

Holiday Care Service, 2 Old Bank Chambers, Horley, Surrey. Tel: 02934 74535.

Holiday Inn Weekenders, 10–12 New College Parade, Finchley Road, London NW3. Tel: 01 586 8111.

Hoseasons Holidays, Sunway House, Lowestoft, Norwich. Tel: 0502 87373.

Hoverspeed, Maybrook House, Queens Gardens, Dover. Tel: 0304 214514 or 01 554 7061.

Interhomes, 383 Richmond Road, Twickenham, Middlesex. Tel: 01 891 1294.

Inter-Hotel, 35 Hogarth Road, London SW5. Tel: 01 373 3241.

International Teddy Bear Club, Trocadero Centre, Piccadilly, London W1. Tel: 01 437 6706.

Irish Farm Holidays Association, Ashton Grove, Knockraha, Co. Cork.

Kiddy Mail, Vinces Road, Diss, Norfolk. Tel: 0379 4720.

Kuoni Travel, Kuoni House, Dorking, Surrey. Tel: 0306 881002.

La Manga Club (Spain), Silver City House, 62 Brompton Road, London SW3. Tel: 01 225 0411.

Ladbroke Holidays, Caister Holiday Centre, Caister, Great Yarmouth, Norfolk. Tel: 0493 720243.

Ladbroke Hotels, PO Box 137, Millbuck House, Clarendon Road, Watford, Herts. Tel: 0923 38877.

Lancaster Family First, 29/31 Elmfield Road, Bromley, Kent. Tel: 01 697 8181.

Landmark Trust, Shottesbrooke, Maidenhead, Berks. Tel: 0628 82 5925.

Magic of Italy, 47 Shepherds Bush Green, London W12. Tel: 01 743 9900.

Matthews Holidays, 8 Bishopsmead Parade, East Horsley, Leatherhead, Surrey. Tel: 04865 4044.

Meon Villa Holidays, Meon House, Petersfield, Hampshire GU32 3JN. Tel: Petersfield (0730) 66561.

Millfield School, Village of Education, Street, Somerset. Tel: 0458 42291.

National Caravan Council, Catherine House, Victoria Road, Aldershot, Hants.

National Trust Holiday Cottages, 36 Queen Anne's Gate, London SW1. Tel: 01 222 9251.

Neilson Ski, Holiday House, Domestic Road, Leeds. Tel: 0532

434077 or 01 202 2211.

Norway Line, Tyne Commission Quay, Albert Edward Dock, North Shields, Tyne & Wear. Tel: 0632 585555.

Norwegian State Railways Travel Bureau, 21 Cockspur Street, London SW1. Tel: 01 930 6666.

Peltours, Mappin House, 4 Winsley Street, London W1. Tel: 01 580 0372.

Peter Stuyvesant Travel, 7 Percy Street, London W1. Tel: 01 631 3278.

PGL, Station Street, Ross on Wye, Herefordshire. Tel: 0989 65556.

P & O Cruises, Canberra House, 47 Middlesex Street, London E1. Tel: 01 283 8080.

Pontin's Holidays, Bridge Street, Banbury, Oxon. Tel: 0202 295600.

Quality International, Freepost, London SW1. Tel: 01 439 2811.

Queens Moat Houses, Queens Moat House, St Edward's Way, Romford, Essex. Tel: 0708 25814.

Rainbow Mini Holidays, Ryedale Building, Piccadilly, York. Tel: 0904 643355.

Royal Caribbean, Bishops Palace House, 2A Riverside Walk, Kingston upon Thames. Tel: 01 541 5570.

Scanhomes (see Scanscape).

Scanscape Holidays, 197–9 City Road, London EC4. Tel: 01 251 2500.

Serena Holidays (see Club Valtur).

SkiNat, Holiday House, Domestic Road, Leeds. Tel: 0532 434077.

Small World, Old Stone House, Judges Terrace, East Grinstead, Sussex. Tel: 0342 27272.

SNCF French Railways, 179 Piccadilly, London W1V 0BA. Tel: 01 409 1224 (Motorail: 409 3518).

Speedwing, 60 Marylebone Lane, London W1. Tel: 01 486 8371.

SPLASH, Empire House, Clarence Street, Swindon, Wilts. Tel: 0793 613220.

Stardust & Camelot, Kiln House, 210 New Kings Road, London SW6. Tel: 01 736 5500.

Sunsites Ltd, Sunsites House, Dorking, Surrey. Tel: 0306 887733.

Superbreak Mini Holidays, 305 Gray's Inn Road, London WC1. Tel: 01 278 0383.

Superstar Holidays, 193 Regent Street, London W1. Tel: 01 439 0126.

Tjaereborg, 7–8 Conduit Street, London W1. Tel: 01 499 8676.

Tradewinds, Faraway House, 66/68 Brewer Street, London W1. Tel: 01 734 1260.

Travel Club of Upminster, Station Road, Upminster, Essex. Tel: 040 22 25000.

Virgin Holidays, Saxon House, Stephenson Way, Crawley, West Sussex. Tel: 0293 775511.

Wings-OSL, Broxbourne, Herts. Tel: 0992 87233.

Wyndham Hotels, Morris Kevan Assoc., Chase Green House, 42 Chase Side, Enfield, Middlesex.

Britain: Tourist Boards

The English Tourist Board, Thames Tower, Black's Road, Hammersmith, London W6 9EL. Tel: 01 846 9000.

Scottish Tourist Board, 23 Ravelston Terrace, Edinburgh EH4 3EU. Tel: 031 332 2433.

Wales Tourist Board, Brunel House, 2 Fitzalan Road, Cardiff CF2 1UY. Tel: 0222 499909. Also: 34 Piccadilly, London W1. Tel: 01 409 0969.

Cumbria Tourist Board, Holly Road, Ashleigh, Windermere, Cumbria LA23 2AQ. Tel: 09662 4444/7. (Cumbria)

East Anglia Tourist Board, Toppesfield Hall, Hadleigh, Suffolk IP7 5DN. Tel: 0473 822922. (Norfolk, Suffolk, Essex and Cambridgeshire)

East Midlands Tourist Board, Exchequergate, Lincoln LN2 1PZ. Tel: 0522 31521/3. (Derbyshire, Leicestershire, Lincolnshire, Northamptonshire and Nottinghamshire)

Heart of England Tourist Board, Old Bank House, Bank Street, Worcester WR1 2EW. Tel: 0905 29511. (Gloucestershire, Herefordshire, Shropshire, Staffordshire, Warwickshire, Worcestershire and West Midlands)

London Visitor and Convention Bureau, 26 Grosvenor Gardens, London SW1W 0DU. Tel: 01 730 3450. (The Greater London Area)

Northumbria Tourist Board, 9 Osborne Terrace, Jesmond, Newcastle upon Tyne NE2 1NT. Tel: 0632 817744. (Cleveland, Durham, Northumberland, Tyne & Wear)

North West Tourist Board, The Last Drop Village, Bromley Cross, Bolton, Lancs BL7 9PZ. Tel: 0204 591511. (Cheshire, Greater Manchester, Lancashire, Merseyside and the High Peak District of Derbyshire)

South East England Tourist Board, 1 Warwick Park, Tunbridge Wells, Kent TN2 5TA. Tel: 0892 40766. (East Sussex, Kent, Surrey, West Sussex)

Southern Tourist Board, The Town Hall Centre, Leigh Road, Eastleigh, Hants. SO5 4DE. Tel: 0703 616027. (Hampshire, Eastern Dorset and the Isle of Wight)

Thames and Chilterns Tourist Board, 8 The Market Place, Abingdon, Oxon OX14 3HG. Tel: 0235 22711. (Oxfordshire, Berkshire, Bedfordshire, Buckinghamshire and Hertfordshire)

West Country Tourist Board, Trinity Court, 37 Southernhay East, Exeter EX1 1QS. Tel: 0392 76351. (Avon, Cornwall, Devon, Western Dorset, Somerset, Wiltshire, The Isles of Scilly)

Yorkshire and Humberside Tourist Board, 312 Tadcaster Road, York YO2 2HF. Tel: 0904 707961. (Humberside, North Yorkshire, West Yorkshire, South Yorkshire)

Abroad: National Tourist Boards

Austrian National Tourist Office, 30 St George Street, London W1R 0AL. Tel: 01 629 0461.

Belgian National Tourist Office, 38 Dover Street, London W1X 3RB. Tel: 01 499 5379.

Tourism Canada, Canada House, Trafalgar Square, London SW1Y 5BJ. Tel: 01 629 9492.

Cyprus Tourism Organisation, 213 Regent Street, London W1R 8DA. Tel: 01 734 9822/2593.

The Danish Tourist Board, 169/173 Regent Street, London W1R 8PY. Tel: 01 734 2637.

Florida Division of Tourism, Suite I, 55 Park Lane, London W1Y 3DH. Tel: 01 493 1343.

French Government Tourist Office, 178 Piccadilly, London W1V 0AL. Tel: 01 491 7622.

German National Tourist Office, 61 Conduit Street, London W1R 0EN. Tel: 01 734 5853.

Greek National Tourist Organization, 195/197 Regent Street, London W1R 8DL. Tel: 01 734 5997.

Bord Failte—Irish National Tourist Board, Ireland House, 150 New Bond Street, London W1Y 0AQ. Tel: 01 493 3201.

Israel Government Tourist Office, 18 Great Marlborough Street, London W1V 1AF. Tel: 01 434 3651.

Italian State Tourist Office, ENIT, 1 Princes Street, London W1R 8AY. Tel: 01 408 1254.

Jamaica Tourist Board, 50 St James's Street, London SW1A 1JT. Tel: 01 493 1707/8.

Malta National Tourist Office, College House, Wrights Lane, London W8 5SH. Tel: 01 938 2668.

Moroccan National Tourist Office, 174 Regent Street, London W1R 6HB. Tel: 01 437 0073.

Netherlands Board of Tourism, 25—28 Buckingham Gate, London SW1E 6LD. Tel: 01 828 4941.

State of New York Division of Tourism, 25 Bedford Square, London WC1B 3HG. Tel: 01 323 0648/9.

Norwegian Tourist Board, 20 Pall Mall, London SW1Y 5NE. Tel: 01 839 2650.

Portuguese National Tourist Office, 1/5 New Bond Street, London W1Y 0NP. Tel: 01 493 3873.

Spanish National Tourist Office, 57/58 St James Street, London SW1A 1LD. Tel: 01 499 0901.

Swedish National Tourist Office, 3 Cork Street, London W1X 1HA. Tel: 01 437 5816.

Swiss National Tourist Office, Swiss Centre, New Coventry Street, London W1V 8EE. Tel: 01 734 1921.

Tunisian National Tourist Office, 7a Stafford Street, London W1X 4EQ. Tel: 01 499 2234.

The Turkish Tourism Information Office, 170/173 Piccadilly, London W1V 9DD. Tel: 01 734 8681/2.

United States Travel Service, 22 Sackville Street, London W1X 2EA. Tel: 01 439 7433.

Yugoslav National Tourist Office, 143 Regent Street, London W1R 8AE. Tel: 01 734 5243.

INDEX

abroad 10−12, 31−5, 55−68
accommodation 36−9, 83−90
  abroad 37, 87−90
  guidebooks 87
  hotel chains 83−90
  UK 36, 83−7
  also see hotels
activity holidays
  families 50, 119−22
  teenagers 28
  unaccompanied children 44−5,
    123−8
aircraft 146
  breastfeeding on 146−7
  facilities on 146−8
airfares 143
airlines 146−9
airports 143−4
air travel 141−2
  disabled children 136
  earache 162
  in pregnancy 158
  jetlag 163
  travel sickness 162−3
alone 42−5

b&b's 37−8
babies 15−19
  shopping abroad 174−8
babyfood abroad 176−8
babymilk abroad 177
babyseats, carhire 152
babysitting 19, 40−1
  miniclubs abroad 69−71
Balearics 56
beaches 72−5
  best beaches 73−5
  pollution on 72−3
bikes 60, 64, 157
bites 164−5
boating 82
booking addresses 192−8
books 171−3
  reference 190

breastfeeding 17
  on planes 146
  on trains 155
Britain 49−55
British Visitor's Passport 185
buggy 18, 146

camping 107−11
  abroad 108−11
  UK 107−8
caravanning 107−11
  abroad 108−11
  UK 107−8
carhire
  abroad 152
  babyseats 152
Caribbean 56−7
carrycots
  on planes 147
car travel 150−3
  all inclusive holidays 153−4
cassette tapes
  for travelling 153
circus schools 116
cities 92
Club Méditerranée 116−17
conservation 130
cots 18−19, 21
country by country 49−68
crèches 19, 119−21, 143
  also see nurseries
creeping eruption 165
cruises 81−2
cuts 165

day camps 44−5, 123−5
Denmark 57
  hotels 89
diarrhoea 159−61
discounts 24, 27−8, 33
  at hotels 84−6, 88−90
  for single parents 134
  on airfares 143
  on ferries 153−6

on trains 155−7
Disneyland 66−7
disposable nappies 174−5
driving
    abroad 151−3
    babyseats 152
    packing up 153
    regulations 151
    seatbelt laws 151
    UK 150−1

earache on planes 162−3
England 49−52
    hotels 83−6
    seasides 29−30
    theme parks 50−2
equipment 18, 22, 180−3
European holidays 55−68

family holidays
    activity, sports 119−22
    beaches 74−5
farms 37, 102−6
    abroad 105−6
    UK 37−8, 102−5
ferries 153−5
film 178−9
five's to eleven's 25−7
food
    abroad 31, 96−7, 178
    at airports 144
    at service stations 150−1
    on planes 147−8
Form E111 187−8
France 59
    by train 156−7
    hotels 88
free holidays 34, 55, 57, 84,
        86−90, 98, 110, 154−5

games 171−3
Germany 59−60
    farms 106
    hotels 89
gîtes 59, 98, 105, 154
Greece 60
guesthouses 37
guidebooks 190−1
    UK hotels and seasides 87

handicapped children 135−8
hazards 21, 169−70
health 159−68
holiday camps 24, 112−14
holiday clubs and centres
    abroad 114−18

holiday contacts 192−8
holiday ideas 47−68
Holland 60−1
hot climates 163−4
hotels
    abroad 37, 87−90
    chains 83−90
    discounts 28, 55, 84−6, 88−90
    guidebooks 87
    sharing rooms 33−4, 83−90
    UK 36, 83−6

ideas for holidays 47−68
immunisation 77, 165−7
information 139−58
insurance 186−9
    discounts for families 188
Ireland 61
    farms 106
Israel 61−2
    hotels 89
    kibbutz 106
Italy 62−3
    farms 106

jetlag 163
journeys 144−6, 148, 150, 153

kibbutz 106
kindergartens 55
    skiing 79−80
    also see individual countries,
        miniclubs and nurseries

language books 172
Legoland 57−8
long distances 34−5, 76−8, 163

malaria 158, 167−8
medical kit 182
medicines abroad 178
    first aid kit 182−3
milk for babies abroad 177−8
miniclubs abroad 69−71
    tour operators 70−1
    also see country by country
        entries
mosquito bites 164−5
motorail 157
motoring holidays 150−3
    road safety 151
motorways 151−2
    services 150−1

nappies
 availability and prices abroad
  174−5
 nappy rash 164
 on planes 147
national tourist boards 197−8
Norway 63−4
 hotels 89
nurseries: see holiday camps,
  holiday clubs and
  centres, package tours
  and skiing

package tours 32−4, 69−71
 hotels 37
 longhaul and winter sun 77−8
 miniclubs 69−71
 prices and discounts 33
packing 180−3
 bags 181−3
 first aid kit 182
 for journeys 146, 181
 self-catering 182
passports 184−6
 for teddy bears 185−6
photography 14
 film 178−9
Portugal 64
potty, inflatable 181
pregnancy
 falling ill abroad 168
 insurance in 188−9
 travel in 157−8, 167
prices 24, 27, 33
 at hotels 84−6
 for single parents 134
 on ferries 153−6
 on trains 155−7
prickly heat 164
pubs 86−7

reference books 190−1
residential camps 45, 125−8
road safety 151

Scandinavia 57−9, 63−4, 64−5
 hotels 89
Scotland 54−5
seaside 29, 30
seatbelt laws 151
self-catering 38−9, 93−101
 abroad 96−100
 packing 100−1
 UK 94−6
ships 153−5
shopping abroad 174−9

short breaks 91−2, 113
sightseeing 13, 121
single parents 42−3, 132−4
skiing 79−80
 also see country by country
  entries
skycots 147−8
Sol Hotels 89
Spain 64
 hotels 89
special interest 119−21
sports 119−22
 unaccompanied children
  124−8
stings 164−5
sunburn, heatstroke 163−4
Sweden 64−5
 hotels 89
Switzerland 65
 hotels 89

taking it in 8−13
teenagers 27−8
theme parks 50−2
three to five's 22−5
toddlers 19−22
touring 150−3
 all inclusive holidays 153−5
tourist boards, offices 196−8
tour operators
 addresses 192−5
 hotels 37
 longhaul and winter sun 34,
  77−8
 miniclubs 69−71
 package holidays 32−5, 69−71
 self-catering 98−100
trains 155−7
travelling 139−58
 by air 141−9, 162−3
  colds 162
  earache 162
  jetlag 163
 by car 150−3
  sickness 161−2
 by ship 153−5
  seasickness 161−2
 by train 155−7
 during pregnancy 157−8
travel sickness 161−2

unaccompanied children's
 holidays 44−5, 123−8
unaccompanied young flyers 149
USA 66−8
 Disney 66−7

hotels 90

vaccinations 77, 165–7
  centres 167
  in pregnancy 157–8

Wales 53–4
where to stay 36–9
winter sun 76–8
working holidays 129–31

Yugoslavia

REPORT FORM

TO: SUSAN GROSSMAN, *Have Kids, Will Travel*
Christopher Helm Publishers,
Imperial House,
21–25 North Street,
Bromley, Kent BR1 1SD.

From my personal experience the following holiday
should/should not be included in future editions of this
book:

....

....

....

....

Address/Tour operator/Country ....

....

....

Tel No: ....   Date of visit ....

Please give full details of suitability/unsuitability for
families.

....

....

please continue over the page

....

....

....

....

Children's comments on holiday:
(Please give any amusing, interesting quotes from children, give age.)

....

....

....

....

....

....

....

....

I am in no way connected with the holiday company/
hotel.

Name and address ....

....

....

Signed ....

REPORT FORM

TO: SUSAN GROSSMAN, *Have Kids, Will Travel*
Christopher Helm Publishers,
Imperial House,
21–25 North Street,
Bromley, Kent BR1 1SD.

From my personal experience the following holiday
should/should not be included in future editions of this
book:

....

....

....

....

Address/Tour operator/Country ....

....

....

Tel No: ....   Date of visit ....

Please give full details of suitability/unsuitability for
families.

....

....

please continue over the page

....

....

....

....

Children's comments on holiday:
(Please give any amusing, interesting quotes from children, give age.)

....

....

....

....

....

....

....

....

I am in no way connected with the holiday company/
hotel.

Name and address ....

....

....

Signed ....